I0463737

ADVANCE PRAISE

Terri Kabachnick has specialized in helping companies develop people and their top assets for decades. Creative and eye-opening, this book is a perfect complement to her last book "I Quit But Forgot to Tell You". This new book is essential for leaders to explore their internal drive, passion, and continuous focus to "Love what they do". Just read it and you will be glad you did.

Ed Peterson, General Manager –
TTM Technologies, Inc. – Silicon Valley

I have seen the results of the concepts that Terri writes about in her book over the last few years at a number of our manufacturing divisions throughout North America. Terri has brought a very unique set of skills and expertise in coaching and training key personnel in our facilities. This book is a must read for any executive, manager, or supervisor who wants to get the most out of an energized and engaged workforce while driving their organization to operational excellence!

Steven N. Lach, Sr. Vice President –
Specialty Business Unit – Viasystems Technologies, LLC

I appreciate Terri's writing because it is well researched with practical applications. However, what I enjoy most is the clear passion she has to lead us to own and love our work. She is a profound voice that leaders, executives and all of us need to learn from on an increasingly global stage."

Ron Price, Founder, President and CEO –
Price Associates

Reading Terri Kabachnick's latest book is like chatting with your own private life coach over coffee. Her conversational style goes down easy, but underneath, the messages in her book are pointed, powerful and personal. Inspiring a look in the self-discovery mirror, Terri persuades you to pinpoint what REALLY lights your fire, and then urges you to pursue it. Laced with research-based truths, this quick-read will focus your personal clarity to take the "right" action…no small feat in today's dizzily complex workplace.

**Deborah "Mickey" Lord, Director of Talent Management –
Roofing Supply Group, LLC – Dallas, Texas**

Read this book because it captures the importance of self-awareness. Self-awareness is the breakfast of champions, and most successful people use self-awareness to build relationships that last.

**Bill Bonnstetter, Founder and Chairman –
Target Training International – Scottsdale, AZ**

Improving the human work experience has long been a passion of mine, and this book will give you the road map to empower yourself and those you lead. Regardless of rank and file, we all lead many more people than we realize, and every moment that we actively engage in the nuances of our own lives, we are leading by example. It does all, however, start with leading yourself!

There are many programs, seminars and certifications that all promise to deliver the life you want. Here's an authentic way to empower yourself to be an engaging and congruent human being, both as a productive professional and a compassionate fellow (wo)man. Having worked with Terri for over a decade, I have seen the results of allowing people to connect with their authentic selves in the work place, and re-engage their skills to produce the results an organization needs to grow. Finally, in this book people are taught to be their very best selves, in all the facets of their lives.

**Charlotte Matityahu, Former CFO –
Net Optics, Inc.**

Reading through the chapters of "Own What You Do and Love It Too" feels like you are sitting in a room speaking directly with Terri. She combines years of observation, research, and testing to provide a practical guide to today's employer-employee relationship. Her unique insight into understanding generational issues, and harnessing those differences help people find passion in their jobs, and to create that passion in others.

John Sigsbury, President –
SSM Health St. Mary's Hospital – Centralia, IL

I have been in the accounting, tax preparation and small business consulting service for 38 years. Terri and I have been each other's client for about 15 years. We believe that every person is born with a special talent that supersedes that of most other people and if they follow that as their vocation, they will find happiness in their job or small business ownership. This path also makes it easier for them to reach their financial success.

We have worked extensively using two main online assessment reports. First, an assessment that helps people find their niche in life. The second profile assessment explains all of their personality traits on how they should deal with people and how other people should deal with them. I'm always amazed how Terri can help direct people towards their happiness and success instead of simply talking about theory and leaving it up to them to find their own "thing". Clients using these assessments always say they are over 90% accurate. Terri helps employers, small and large, hire the right employees and build their company teams by matching people to the jobs. This book will help everyone within a company begin the process of owning what they do and finding their passion.

Terri is definitely making the world better.

Doug Davenport, Owner –
Developing Business Solutions, LLC

Own What You Do

and

Love it Too

FOR ANYONE WHO
WORKS FOR ANYONE

TERRI KABACHNICK

Archway Publishing books may be ordered through booksellers or by contacting:

Archway Publishing
1663 Liberty Drive
Bloomington, IN 47403
www.archwaypublishing.com
1 (888) 242-5904

Because of the dynamic nature of the Internet, any web addresses or links contained in this book may have changed since publication and may no longer be valid. The views expressed in this work are solely those of the author and do not necessarily reflect the views of the publisher, and the publisher hereby disclaims any responsibility for them.

Any people depicted in stock imagery provided by Thinkstock are models, and such images are being used for illustrative purposes only.
Certain stock imagery © Thinkstock.

ISBN: 978-1-4808-3376-0 (sc)
ISBN: 978-1-4808-3378-4 (hc)
ISBN: 978-1-4808-3377-7 (e)

Library of Congress Control Number: 2016910878

Print information available on the last page.

Archway Publishing rev. date: 08/16/2016

Dedication

I DEDICATE THIS BOOK TO PHIL KABACHNICK –
My husband of 36 years who passed away on February 23, 2014.

Phil was a tremendous influence on me and an incredible guiding light in my life. He taught me the importance of owning what you do—challenging yourself—and loving what you do in spite of the barriers and obstacles that we encounter daily. In all the years that we spent together he encouraged me—understood the hectic pace of my work and life—never complained when I was gone—sometimes for weeks at a time doing what my business demanded of me. He loved me unconditionally—constantly supported me—encouraged me—defended me—made sure I stayed on track—and most important HE BELIEVED IN ME.

I miss you Kabby every single day!!!

Acknowledgements

Over the years, I have been fascinated by people who stayed in jobs they weren't suited for and complained to anyone who would listen about how they couldn't stand the people they worked with. These people went home upset and angry and couldn't muster the energy to face another day at work. These folks were not fun to be with and when they complained, I would sometimes ask, why don't you do something about it? Their excuses were difficult to grasp. They ranged from humorous "it's too hard to find something else" to depressing "who's going to hire me at his point"?

As I began to understand their disenchantment with their job, I realized that in many cases it really wasn't so much about the job as it was about their perceived lack of control. The lack of control over what they did and how they interacted with the people they worked with. This is true for senior executives, supervisors, and entry-level managers.

My purpose in writing this book is partly due to the question I'm so often asked by business owners and corporate executives: "Why don't people embrace and own what they do and be passionate about their work and just be happy?" Other comments I have often heard are ones that blame others for how miserable they are because they can't count on people to give them what they need to do their jobs.

I'm tough on the people that I coach, involve in my workshops, and mentor. I often repeat that you have more control over your work and your workplace than you think you do. Why don't you decide to go for it and make your work an exciting and delicious part of your life? It's a mind set and no one but you have control over your thoughts, your beliefs, and your behaviors.

My book is the result of many people's efforts. People who stood by me, supported me, encouraged me, and guided me.

First and foremost, my heartfelt thanks to my cherished friend and editor Bette Price. This book would not have been possible without Bette's guidance, valid critiques, and honest evaluation. Bette it's a privilege to have known you for so many years and shared so many experiences.

A big thanks go to my dear friend, mentor, and business partner Bill Bonnstetter. Bill's assessments and tools have helped guide my work over the past 25 years that we have known each other. These tools have in turn helped me coach and advise so many people and direct them towards their pursuit of happiness. Thank you is not enough Bill—I love you!

Karen Glass, my Director of Client Communications, deserves huge recognition for her support, dedication, and commitment—especially during my trying times over the past 3 years. Karen you are terrific and I appreciate all that you have done to allow me to make this book happen.

Hugs and thank you to all my friends and business advisors—TTI Valued Associates (you know who you are) and most of all Marjorie Brody, Brian Lee, Ed Oakley, Bob Romano, and Barbara SanFilippo. Love you!

And of course my gratitude to all my clients, many of whom have become dear friends. Thank you for your ongoing encouragement, support and belief in me, and the work that we accomplish together.

CONTENTS

Introduction

The statistics are startling. 54 percent of employed Americans are unhappy with their jobs. Narrow that group to the millennial generation - those ages 18-29 - who are just beginning their careers, and the percentage jumps even higher. More than 70 percent say they are not happy with their current jobs. The problem isn't just in the United States it's a global issue. I consider this an epidemic.

What's up with all this unhappiness?

I contend that it's all about love. That's right. L O V E!

What's love got to do with it? Everything! Because if you don't love what you do you'd better ask yourself:

- What kind of parent are you?
- What kind of spouse are you?

- What kind of friend are you?
- What kind of manager are you?
- What kind of neighbor are you?
- What kind of *you* are you?

Regardless of who you are and what you do, this book is for you and anyone who works for anyone. It doesn't matter what your age is or how new or invested you are in your job. It doesn't matter if you're an employee in a manufacturing plant, a retail store, a self-employed consultant, an Executive or business owner - it really doesn't matter. What is important is that to be truly happy in life and be the best that you can be, you've got to **love what you do**.

Loving what you do creates passion. You can't hide passion. It lives in every pore of your being. It becomes your core—your foundation. Most importantly, passion is something no one can take away from you—you control it.

So, what are you passionate about? Here's a process to help you figure it out:

- Think about how you feel when you're doing something you really enjoy.
- Now reverse that and think about the feelings you have when you're doing something you don't enjoy—something that's really a chore.
- When does time pass by quickly and things just seem to flow? What are the times that despite having worked hard all day, you still feel energized, happy and satisfied because of the accomplishments you've made?

- When does time drag and frustration set in? When does procrastination take over and all of a sudden instead of focusing on the tasks you need to accomplish, you're finding other tasks instead?

Most "mentally healthy" adults naturally want to do a good job—to be proud of what they do and feel they are contributing. This is the essence of motivation. Many people also want to feel they are extremely capable at what they do regardless of the role they play. They could be toll collectors, mail carriers, flight attendants, store managers, business owners, executives, even CEOs. Because it is not about *what* you do, it's all about how you do it. You are the only one that can accurately read your passion meter.

How does a toll collector on the Pinellas Bayway Bridge in Florida show how much he enjoys his job? He takes my toll, greets me with a smile and suggests that I smile all day too. His enthusiasm makes my day. It energizes his as well. Why does one American Airlines flight attendant put a fresh flower in the lavatory when another attendant doesn't? And, where did she get that flower? She obviously took the time to bring the flower with her because she wanted to do something different—something that would add just a little touch of difference for the passengers on her flight.

What does a Chico's store manager do that makes me return to her store when I could easily go to another Chico's closer to where I live? She always takes the time to show sincere concern about my needs and that makes me feel special. None of these people could do the little extra things that they do if they didn't have a passion for what they do.

I recognize that some people will say that many of today's workers don't necessarily want to bond with their job and love what they do—they just want a job. They may also contend that one's job shouldn't be intermingled with one's personal life. It may be healthier to keep the two separate. They'll point out that very few people in today's world expect to work in the same place for any length of time. All these may be reasonable comments, but I say that rationale is flawed. Does it really make sense that regardless of how long you stay at any one company that you'd want to be miserable and hate the work you do? Besides, who ever said that loving what you do is about loyalty or longevity or generational mindsets? Quite frankly it's not even about bosses or salaries. What it is about is values, passions, and connectivity. It's about the emotional connection an employee has to the company and that emotional connection only happens, when the company culture and the employee have shared values, standards, and ethics. When these three elements exist a bond develops. This bond can last for a few years or a few decades, yet once developed it is solid—you can count on it. Many companies already know this. It's a strategy they use in capturing and keeping customers. Unfortunately, far too few companies use the same strategy to capture happy, productive employees.

Passionate Vision

There is a vision that I am personally passionate about: **To get everyone to love what they do.**

As you read this you are probably raising an eyebrow and thinking to yourself, "Good luck, Terri!" That's okay. I've heard comments that are far more skeptical, even downright negative, citing every reason you can think of about why this is an impossible vision to accomplish.

Throughout this book you will read about many of those reasons and you'll begin to see why they don't deter me. You'll see I'm driven by a role model—a visionary man who accomplished what he set out to do even though he was faced with similar skepticism and negativity.

More than thirty years ago Bill Gates said, "There will be a personal computer on every desk and in every home." This seemed like an unreasonable, unachievable statement at the time. But fast-forward to today. Not only is there just one computer on every desk and in every home—there are many.

I, like Bill Gates, fervently believe that my vision is doable. It's doable because I already know of many people who have achieved it—they absolutely love what they do. They have put themselves in the right place with the right opportunities to draw upon their passion and to bond with what they do. They have found this happiness by forming and sharing a bond with a company for which they work and for a brand they have chosen to live every day. Others have found it within their own businesses. Whatever the connection, it is a brand whose vision and mission supports their personal vision or mission. When you think about it, that's why visions or missions are so big. They're big because they need to be propelled with a passion—a belief that what you set out to accomplish will actually come true.

I realize that loving what you do may be a BIG vision or mission, but in each chapter I am giving you an "Own It" guide to help you control your destination. At times it may seem to be taking a little longer than you expected to reach your destination. But, I promise you that your life will never be the same once you achieve that mission and begin loving what you do.

I think about Steve Jobs. He was fired from Apple, the company he helped found. "It was awful tasting medicine," Jobs told a graduating class at Stanford. "But I guess the patient needed it. Sometimes life hits you in the head with a brick. Don't lose faith. I'm convinced that the only thing that kept me going was that I loved what I did. You've got to find what you love. This is as true for your work as it is for your lovers. Your work is going to fill a large part of your life, and the only way to be truly satisfied is to do what you believe is great work. The only way to do great work is to love what you do. If you haven't found it yet—keep looking."

I'm writing this book to help you do exactly that. Think of the reality. Life is too short to miss one moment of all the love and joy you are entitled to. Yet, to do that, you have to be willing to be responsible for controlling the environments you choose so that they nurture and foster the very best in you. In this book, I'll help you explore all the elements that go into ensuring you put yourself in the types of environments that provide the right opportunities to love what you do so you can also own what you do. Regardless of your role in life—be it Contributor (an hourly or line employee), Manager (one who manages other people or processes), Executive (those with wide areas of responsibilities and substantial budgets to manage) or Leader (those who create the mission and vision for their enterprises and are the ultimate decision-makers)—this book is for you. Let's get started.

> *When you identify with your company's purpose – when you experience ownership in a shared vision – you'll find yourself doing your life's work instead of just doing time.*
>
> SOURCE UNKNOWN

CHAPTER ONE

The Seductive Interview

Much like a first date, forming a bond and building the foundation for loving what you do happens on the first date— the interview. The interview is that critical moment when either love begins or the stage is set for future disappointment. This is the case whether the interview is for an entirely new job at a new company, a lateral move for the same job at a new company, or a promotion within the company you may already love. Just because you love your current job and the company, doesn't mean you can ignore this interview stage when it involves a promotion or any other type of move. All interviews are critical moments. But, for today's purposes, let's focus on the initial interview for a brand new job; a job that sounds like it is ideally suited to you, your talents and your aspirations.

Imagine that based on your resume, your references, and experience the company has already decided that you not only look good – as in qualified – you really are good. Your future boss wants to make sure you accept the job so it's now important for the interviewer to do whatever it takes to be sure he convinces you. In other words, the interviewer has to sell you on the company and the great opportunities that the position will provide for you.

Suddenly the seduction begins.

Let me share with you a real situation; an interview I was able to sit in on. It went like this:

Hello, Michelle. Let me begin by telling you a little about our company. The first thing I'd like you to know is that we're a very people focused company; our people are our greatest asset. Everything we do here is done with our people in mind.

We are also a team-centered organization. No one individual stands alone. We believe in and reward teamwork. At the same time we also reward our people for their individual contributions and their creativity. So, we look for people who are able to interact with their co-workers, build strong relationships, and at the same time, always be on the lookout for how they can help improve their jobs and further the mission of the company. We listen and we react.

Your job as a store manager will focus on the people aspects— your associates and your customers. As you know, both are critical to the store's success. If you can lead your associates—motivate them—and develop them, our customers will benefit from those results and reward us with their business.

Right now you will have a great team to work with and I know you can take them to even new heights.

Michelle, how does this picture of our company fit with what you'd like to do and where you'd like to work?

How does this scenario resemble an interview you may have had? Were you ever sold on the job based on the interviewer's glorious descriptions of the company, the people, and the rewards of the job itself? Now the big question: Was it the truth?

To see if it was the truth for Michelle, let's follow her journey and fast-forward six months as we eavesdrop on Michelle's conversation with her boss, Dan, the District Manager:

Dan, I just want you to know how excited I was when I started this job. I had so many ideas to help improve our store and our business. But, now I'm finding that nothing I say matters. I'm supposed to follow orders, do what I must do everyday, and as you've told me, not to worry so much about my people. What I've learned is most important is that I get all the reports in on time and focus on following the directions for visual and markdowns.

I feel like a robot—but more importantly, I'm now being blamed for associate turnover. Dan, I have no time for my associates and I have no time at all for customers—unless there's a major complaint. I have no interaction with the merchants other than when they come in to tell me what's wrong. Had I had any clue that this was the job I was taking I never would have applied.

No one takes a job with the intention of failing. No manger hires with the intent to fire.

So, what happens in a case like this? It begins at the beginning— the interview.

By definition, an interview is: "A formal consultation usually to evaluate qualifications (as of a prospective student or employee) 2a: a meeting at which information is obtained (as by a reporter, television commentator, or pollster) from a person."

But, is this really what an interview is?

Having witnessed dozens of these events over the years I have come to believe that today interviews have become selling events. Whether that is because of a talent [not people] shortage, poor training in interviewing skills or simply the compulsion for the interviewer to talk rather than listen, interviews are no longer what they should be.

Interviews should be evaluations of the applicant based on a clear understanding of what the job requires for the applicant to be a success. That means that the competencies, behaviors, and values that prospective candidates bring to the job must match those required by the job. But do they? Do they even come close?

In order for you to love what you do you first have to be in an environment that supports that love, therefore allows it to flourish. Your boss is a critical element of concern because if your boss doesn't love what he does, how will that affect you? Thus, not only does loving what you do require a culture that supports you, but a boss that loves what he does so he can create an environment that supports you. Only then can you begin to *own* what you do.

What could you do to probe deeper and have better insight into the company and your boss? You can do this by asking important questions during your interview with your future boss. Your interview was never meant to be a one-way street—questions can and should flow in both directions, but you must come prepared with the right questions so you don't merely listen and get blindly seduced.

Here are some examples of questions that will provide revealing insights for you, the applicant:

1. What are the three most important non-negotiables that you expect of someone working for you?
2. Could you give me an example of a time when someone working for you made a mistake that affected a customer? How did you handle the situation? What did you say? How did the employee react? What happened a month after the incident?
3. What is your number one hot button?
4. Who in the company do you see as your mentor?
5. Who do you most respect as a leader? Why?
6. Do you mentor anyone? What is the process you use?
7. Have you attended any personal development courses or workshops recently? What were the best things you learned?
8. Who is the person who most influenced your career success? What did he or she teach you?
9. On which tasks or areas do you spend more than fifty percent of your time?
10. What time do you generally arrive at work? What time do you usually leave?
11. What is your preferred method of communication? Example: phone, eMail, face-to-face, text?
12. If you were to tell me just one very important thing that I should know about you, what would that be?
13. What are three adjectives most people would use to describe you?

Granted, most smart bosses will likely have the perfect answers to these questions. However, what you are really looking for is more than just right answers; you are watching for their reactions—their facial expressions—their body language. You're observing how long it takes them to answer a question and to note when they're hesitant. Are they animated when they answer specific questions? This could signal a passion for that specific topic. Do they look frustrated with any question, possibly wondering what right you have for asking it in the first place? That is a telltale indicator as well. Do they begin fidgeting or glancing at their watch? What does that tell you?

The point is, when you ask probing questions and pay attention to not only what is said, but how it's said and the emotional response, you will gain insight into aspects of the job and your boss that are important to you—aspects that you may not have otherwise discovered.

Some of you may be saying "Yeah right! I can just see myself asking these questions. I just want a job!" My response to that is, fine, do you want to find out in six months that you hate your job? Or do you want to make the right decision from the beginning that will eventually impact you and everyone around you?

Your DNA

What would you think might happen if you arrived for an interview—either for a new job at a new company or for a promotion within the company in which you are already employed—armed with a computerized assessment to validate the skills that you have already mastered? An unbiased document that has assessed the skills you have fully developed, somewhat developed, and have yet to develop.

Wouldn't this serve as a great foundation for a solid conversation that would deal with the reality of what you bring to the job? Wouldn't this be useful to compare the skills you have developed to see how well they align with the skills required for the job?

Here's how that might work:

Let's assume that your skills do not match those that the job requires. For example, let's say you're applying for a position in sales. Let's look at the comparison between the skills you have mastered and the skills required for the position:

The skills that you have fully developed include:

1. Planning and Organization
2. Continuous Learning
3. Analytical Problem Solving
4. Negotiation
5. Leadership

The skills that the job requires:

1. Goal Orientation
2. Interpersonal Skills
3. Persuasion
4. Personal Effectiveness
5. Self-Management (time and priorities)

It doesn't take long to see that this may not be the best match for you. So, what do you do? You could decide to conceal the assessment results and go ahead and interview for the job. But, what would be your real chances for achieving success, even if for some strange reason you were offered the job? The reality is that sooner or later you would become disenchanted with the job, thus disengaged. Or, your boss would become dissatisfied with your performance and that could be even worse. Wouldn't it be much better for everyone if you could validate that your skills and the job required skills were a good match to begin with?

Let's assume that your assessment showed that you had mastered these skills instead:

1. Interpersonal Skills
2. Leadership
3. Self-Management
4. Personal Effectiveness
5. Futuristic Thinking

Wow! What a difference. Although it's not an identical match, it's a high percentage of matched skills and the two missing skills could easily be strengthened with coaching. With this strong match there is certainly a greater likelihood that the job fit will be good for both you and your employer.

Validated research has shown that there are 25 personal skills of which several need to be mastered for successful performance in any specific job. Individuals seldom fully develop all 25. What is most important is that the skills the individual has developed are the skills that the job requires for success. If you have developed a skill or skills that the job does not require it may actually be a detriment to being successful in that particular job.

As an example: An individual is applying for a job as a prison guard. Upon reviewing the applicant's DNA assessment the hiring manager discovers that the applicant has high scores in Empathy—Customer Service—Interpersonal Skills—and Flexibility. What do you think his chances for success in the job of a prison guard would be? Matching the job to the person is a critical element in ensuring engagement and success in the position.

As important as all of this is, I must admit that occasionally an individual is so disconnected from reality that it's humorous as to what job they think they might want or whether they would bring any value to it. Here's a case in point:

A woman applied for a store manager's job at Chico's although she had absolutely no experience in retail. Not only did she bring no experience to the position, but she also let the regional manager know that she expected 20 percent more than the salary posted for the position. When the regional manager asked her why—what was she thinking, her response was: "It takes double the effort and more work when you don't know what you're doing."

While admittedly, this is somewhat of a rare occasion it does make the point that having a clear understanding of the skills you bring to a job are important to consider when interviewing for the job, regardless of how seductive the interviewer is.

Own it:

- Mastery of skills depends upon the specific job and the hierarchy of skills the job requires for success. Development of the most important skills required for your personal and professional life is what is critical.
- Would you like to know which skills you have developed? Well you can.

Contact us at www.kabachnick.com and we'll tell you how you can receive a complimentary report on the skills you have developed. This report includes your most important competencies – your preferred behavior patterns, communication and work style preferences – and your values/motivators.

CHAPTER TWO

Passions and Perceptions

Many times the source of unhappiness about a job is simply due to perceptions—feeling that you have to change what you do in order to please a boss, a co-worker, or even a customer. How do you know these changes are necessary if all you have to go by is what you think? When you pinpoint exactly how you feel about what you do, then you can determine the areas to focus on to change, improve, or forget about trying to change.

Many say, "Perception is reality". I say *perception is reality only for the ignorant*. Tough words! But I'll argue that if you don't have the facts, or know the truth, then you are ignorant in your knowledge—and as a result all you have to go on is your perception.

Here's an example:

Michael is a sales person in the highly competitive world of IT — working for a telecommunications company. Michael has been with the company for five years. He's been successful in reaching and surpassing his goals, and also received very good performance reviews. However, recently his boss and some of his co-workers noticed a change in Michael's typically "happy" attitude. His change was described to me as, "The zing is gone". His boss asked me to meet with Michael and to see if I could discover the root cause of the noticeable changes.

When I met with Michael he admitted that he was becoming discouraged and unhappy in his job. It turns out that his unhappiness began recently. I wanted to know more about the reasons—whether this was a perception that Michael had or a true disenchantment with his job or the company. I asked Michael if he would be willing to complete our behavior, competencies, and driving forces assessments and also to take my "Passion Meter" quiz. He agreed. The assessments showed that he was very well matched to the job—had all the behavior characteristics necessary to succeed in his job and his driving forces or motivators were aligned with the job requirements. He also had mastered the skills, which led to all his successes.

So what was the problem? Well, the Passion Meter quiz caught it. It was all about some perceptions that Michael developed related to how he handled long-term customers. It seems that Michael overheard a conversation between the president of the company and his boss.

Here's what Michael heard:

Michael's boss was arguing a point with the president that the customer may not always be right and when the customer becomes too demanding the relationship can become costly and then be compromised—losing the value of that customer to the company. There has to be a win-win. The president was upset by this opinion and told Michael's boss that if a relationship with a long-term customer is ever broken then he will personally "attend" to the person at fault.

Michael always prided himself with the customer relationships he built and maintained with his long-term customers even though sometimes it meant he had to push back when he felt the customer was becoming too demanding. He used his excellent negotiating skills and despite any initial differences he always managed to come to a mutually acceptable agreement. Now after hearing the president's comments Michael began wavering and questioning himself on how far he should push back on a customer the next time it came to a disagreement on costs or delivery times, etc. Michael began operating from fear—which was fully contrary to his natural strengths. He began to worry and doubt his abilities. He also knew that he inherently disagreed with the president's views. Because Michael has a high Utilitarian driving force—which means he greatly values time and money—he always put the interests of the company first. To Michael it's all about winning sales and surpassing goals. Now, Michael's perception took over his reality. No one told Michael to change his approach or in any way alter his style. Michael simply created his own perceptions.

I spoke with Michael's boss in order to clarify what the president truly meant in his comments and explained that a different picture had emerged from what Michael had overheard. It turned out that the reason for the conversation with the president was because the customer called the president and complained about late deliveries and poor communication with their sales representative. But what Michael did not know and did not hear was that this customer was eight months behind in their payments, thus the late deliveries were a result of these poor payments—not Michael's actions. What the president was emphasizing was that there better be a very good reason for losing a long-term customer and he wanted to know about it and be personally involved.

Clarifying the wrong perceptions that Michael held brought a huge sense of relief to him. It also made Michael truly understand that things aren't always what they seem. He also learned a valuable lesson in that his customers could also have poor or wrong perceptions, therefore his job was to always ensure that his customers had all the facts, data, and information they needed in order to make the right decisions. Poor or nonexistent communication leads to ignorance. And where there's a hole left something has to fill it. Perceptions often become the fill. To avoid perceptions requires self-awareness about your passions so you can truly own what you do.

My Passion Meter quiz will help you to determine this.

PASSION METER

Self-awareness is the first step in empowering yourself to avoid perceptions, make decisions and know how to react to and interact with daily challenges and pressures. Being truthful in your assessment of your job and your feelings about your workplace will clarify the actions you need to take to move you to owning what you do. Answer the following questions and/or statements with a "yes" or "no."

1. If money were not a factor, would you do what you do for free?
2. Does your work energize you?
3. Are you still learning and growing?
4. Do you share your thoughts and ideas with others at work?
5. Do you look forward to going to work?
6. Do you have good friends at work?
7. My job makes good use of my skills & abilities.
8. My job is everything I expected it to be.
9. Do you feel respected and liked by the people you interact with?
10. I feel valued as an employee of my company.
11. Are your contributions recognized regularly?
12. Are you passionate about the mission of your organization?
13. My work gives me a feeling of personal accomplishment.
14. Is the feedback that you receive generally positive?
15. Do you feel that your work adds positive value to the organization?
16. I am encouraged to come up with new and better ways of doing things.
17. My boss consistently recognizes me when I do a good job.
18. My boss focuses more on my strengths than my weaknesses.
19. I have received the training I need to do a quality job.

20. Do you have confidence in and respect for your boss?
21. Are you in a position to learn from your boss and will he/she help you advance?
22. The people I work with cooperate together to get the job done.
23. I care so much about my company that I would defend it against criticism.
24. My boss listens to my ideas and concerns.
25. My boss always treats me with respect and dignity.
26. I have a clear understanding of my responsibilities.
27. Do you have control over how you spend your time and what you do?
28. I receive information on a consistent and timely basis from management.
29. I have a strong positive relationship with my boss.
30. Do you admire the organization's leadership?

Score:

23-30 Yes answers – You are in a position of owning what you do and loving it too.

15-22 Yes answers – You should choose 3 of your "No" answers that are important to your ownership of your job and work on improving those issues. (e.g: If you answered NO to #13, ask your boss for opportunities for continued learning to help you grow.) Take ownership of your development. Do not wait for someone to approach you and ask you if you would like to learn more. It's not going to happen!

7-14 Yes answers – You are most likely not owning your job. Are you just allowing things to happen to you? Are you bored? Have you spoken to your boss about your challenges? You may still want to do a good job and stay where you are – but be careful because you're sliding fast into disengagement.

1-6 Yes answers – You are not in a good place. I think you know this. Scoot over to the last chapter in this book for advice on facing reality and moving on.

OWN IT

- How do you feel about what you do?
- Do you see your job for what it truly is or are you viewing it from just your perspective?
- Who can you talk with that will offer a possibly different viewpoint of your job?
- Are you clear about your role or is it merely a perception of the role?
- Are the job accountabilities written and clarified with you?
- Do you have a real passion for what you do?

CHAPTER THREE

Sparing the Sugar and Salt

Do you have self-sabotaging beliefs? Self-sabotaging beliefs are the limiting and negative underlying attitudes and thought patterns that you believe about yourself – your self-perceptions. They impact every area of your life. These self-sabotaging beliefs usually stem from past experiences that influence your route to success. Unfortunately, they may also have nothing to do with who you are now and who you want to be – but they exist. They simply reflect what was.

Ask yourself:

- Do I often doubt what I can accomplish?
- Do I question my ability to get a project completed on time?
- Do I wonder what others may think of me?
- Do I fear the decisions I have to make?

- Do I feel my opinions don't always matter?
- Do I distrust others' desire to help me?

Most everyone I know raises these questions – some often – others once in a while. But at some point we all silently question ourselves. We become our own worst enemy. Then as a result we try to seek the advice of others whom we feel can provide us with some answers. We may view these people as experts or they may position themselves as experts. And so we search for them—and then because some have a very positive outlook we like them. They offer direction, guidance, processes to use, and their knowledge. They'll also offer us encouraging feedback, and friendly support. They are **the sugar**.

Have you ever reached a point when you feel you've failed; when you didn't know if you'd still have your job or be in business? A time when you truly become ill, thinking of what might happen if you can't pay your bills or can't make next week's payroll?

This happened to me in 1990 when all of a sudden I lost several large clients due to the recession. I'll never forget that year. My husband couldn't help me because with the down economy, he was having his own business concerns. So he suggested I call a few people who might be able to help me. I was mortified, embarrassed and angry. Name the emotion; I had it.

Realizing I had little choice I made the most painful phone calls of my life and amazingly, I raised enough money to stay in business. It's no doubt why I'm still in business today.

*Frankly, I was shocked that friends would do this for me. I asked my husband why they would do this. "Because they believe in you—because you believe in you and what you're doing." These people were **the sugar**.*

There are others from whom we seek advice who begin by questioning us—then they critique our direction, our goals, and our work styles. They'll wonder out loud why we've chosen to take on difficult tasks, and why we're aiming for what in their view is impossible. We leave exhausted by these experts. They are **the salt**.

Jennifer had been a flight attendant and had learned a good deal about make-up, poise and fashion. A few years after leaving her job to marry, she was offered a job at a business school that included in its curriculum a course on "Charm and Personality Development." It was a course to help put the finishing touches on its graduates with topics like appropriate dress, dining etiquette and being comfortable speaking in public. Jennifer had no degree to teach, but this particular course did not require one. At the end of the year the school, which had franchises across the country, held a national conference. At the conference various teachers were selected to make presentations. Jennifer was one of the teachers selected to make a presentation regarding her topics.

The last night of the conference an awards dinner was held where a variety of awards were given out with one main award— The Outstanding Teacher of the Year. Much to Jennifer's surprise, when this award was presented, Jennifer's name was called. What an honor, she thought. Out of all these incredible teachers, they gave this award to me.

*Excited about her achievement Jennifer quickly shared her news with a woman from a business organization she belonged to whom she had considered a very good friend. The woman's response was shocking: "Who do you think you are, winning an outstanding teacher award when you don't even have a degree to teach?" She was **the salt.***

How good is everyone's assumed wisdom—the salt or the sugar? Does this "wisdom" answer our needs? That depends on whether you believe that you can help yourself before anyone else can help you. I'm not discussing medical or life issues here. I'm simply arguing that you have more control and power over your thoughts and beliefs than you might think. But you may become overwhelmed at times and as a result don't step back to think clearly and de-stress. Before you run to others for advice – which in my experience you'll get plenty of – consider two things. First, have you given yourself an opportunity to think your issues through? Second, what criteria will you use to get advice from someone?

Let's consider your first option – thinking things through by yourself.

Deepak Chopra, M.D. an alternative medicine advocate, and a promoter of popular forms of spirituality, said in his book <u>Perfect Health,</u> "To change the printout of the body you must learn to rewrite the software of the mind."

If you know something about how your conscious and subconscious mind work this will make more sense. So here are a few things to know:

- Your **subconscious** mind is a storehouse for all of your life experiences, which affect your beliefs, your values, and your attitudes. It's your file cabinet filled with memories.
- Your **subconscious** processes 4 billion bits of information per second – 1000 different thoughts.
- It controls all your motor functions.
- Your **conscious** mind is what you think about and what you want to accomplish.

- However, no matter how hard you try to act on what the conscious mind tells you—the subconscious will always override the conscious mind. In other words, your stored beliefs will win over what your current thoughts are. You want to accomplish something [conscious thoughts] and your subconscious [what's happened before] will say you can't.
- Therefore you must take the time to access your subconscious and discover what's in the storehouse or your filing cabinet.

How do you do that?

In my coaching sessions I often ask the people I'm coaching to do an exercise that has proven to be very valuable and extremely successful over the years. Here's an example of one person's experience.

At the time I started working with Susan she was a determined young lady that had her eyes set on eventually reaching a senior level position at her company. Susan spoke well and had the necessary skills to succeed. However, as time passed she became very negative in her communication and specifically about others' ideas and contributions. Eventually her team and her peers became reluctant to discuss ideas or work issues with her. One person told me that a conversation with Susan felt like having a bucket of ice water thrown at you. Ouch! Not a good comment about a person you should be working with. What many people did not realize and know about Susan is that she had many self-sabotaging and self-doubting beliefs about herself. She frequently believed that she was doomed to fail and compensated for this by attacking other people. Sadly Susan did not see this in herself.

After conducting a 360 review of Susan and then hearing her team members and peers negative comments I asked Susan how she thought others saw her. She thought others saw her as hardworking, dedicated to the mission of the company, and willing to help out when and where needed. I then had Susan revisit her initial goals. Were these goals still ambitions she initially described to me? It turns out they were—Susan still wanted to rise in the company to a senior level. I then explained to her that she would never reach those goals if she continued in her current path. Susan was stunned. She felt that she was contributing to her team's success by expecting the very best from others. She also told me that many times when she caught herself being overly critical she would try to be more positive and to change her negative way of thinking about outcomes. She claimed that no matter how hard she tried somehow the negative thoughts and the anger would come out. In a way this was good news because Susan was somewhat aware of her behavior.

I asked Susan if she truly wanted to change her outlook, her behavior, and her communication style. Did she want to realize her dream of becoming a successful executive? She said she was willing to commit to whatever she needed to do to change and become successful.

Susan then embarked on the "Own It Exercise" (described in Chapter 4). As described in the exercise instructions, once Susan completed the exercise I asked her to put her notes away and not look at them until I felt it was time for her to read them.

After about three weeks I instructed Susan to read her notes and to highlight what she felt were important notations—something she wrote that struck a cord with her. We then reviewed these notes. Susan was quite surprised at some of her observations. She did not understand where these thoughts came from. She then began to see that many of these thoughts came from her upbringing and what she thought about her parents' and teacher's comments to Susan. She began to recognize the long term effect that all of this had on her. Obviously, quite a bit of emotions resulted from this exercise. However, Susan became empowered by this knowledge.

In the course of her newfound knowledge Susan shifted her behaviors and became more transparent with her team and her peers—even asking them for help in her new journey. I am thrilled to divulge that Susan is now in a Director position and moving on up. I still work with her and enjoy seeing her growth.

The next time you consider seeking another's advice, remember to first be confident in your own beliefs. Advice from others will either be sugar or salt and while seeking other's guidance can certainly be helpful when determining your decision path, it will be the most helpful when you are first secure in your own knowledge and beliefs. To ensure that you first give credit to your own beliefs, remember the famous words of Mahatma Gandhi.

"Your beliefs become your thoughts,
Your thoughts become your words,
Your words become your actions,
Your actions become your habits,
Your habits become your values,
Your values become your destiny."

OWN IT:

- Do you seek advice and help from others before you do your homework to understand why you do what you do?
- If you do seek advice—are you looking for the "Salt" or the "Sugar"?
- Do you know others' perceptions of you? Do you ask?
- Record yourself while attending a meeting. How do you sound?
- Are you willing to commit to doing an exercise like the one I suggested to Susan?
- Remember, it's not about you and everyone else. It's about your core beliefs and how you manifest them. What do you believe that no one else believes?

CHAPTER FOUR

Valuing Values

Why don't more companies have employees who love what they do and are passionate about where they work? Why are we blaming turnover and retention problems on generational issues? Why does an executive who works at a fashionable retail company buy her clothes at a competitor's? Why can't more employees love their jobs the way Carol Brooks does—a woman I have highly respected and admired for more than twenty years.

I have discovered that the answer is the same for each question; it quite simply comes down to one thing—SHARED VALUES. When an employee believes that the Values of the company and their jobs match their individual values, a bond with that brand is formed. They are at the core from which the company operates and grows its success. David Walker, former Comptroller General of the United States said it well: "I'm a great believer in core values. They are the beliefs that drive what you do, and they are also boundaries that set up the limit of what you are willing to do."

So just what are Values? We also refer to them as Motivators or Driving Forces. They are your hidden motivators. They are the drivers behind your behavior—what motivates you to do what you do. Values are the principles or standards by which you act. Your Values are the beliefs and passions that you hold very strongly and as a result they affect your thinking and your behavior. We have often heard people ask, "Why does he do what he does?" The key question here is WHY? Our communication and work style preferences tell us HOW we go about doing things. But our Values—our Driving Forces—explain the WHY.

Determining your Driving Forces is an eye opening experience. Understanding yourself and what drives you helps you to understand not just yourself, but others and what drives them. The authority behind this discovery process is Bill Bonnstetter, Founder and Chairman of Target Training International, Ltd. [TTI], the company he founded in 1984. His company develops research-based, validated assessment products that are used in more than 75 countries and 28 languages. His work on the Driving Forces assessment is based on the work of German philosopher and psychologist, Eduard Spranger. Bonnstetter was the first to receive a patent on the personalized reports that integrate the Values and Behaviors of individuals.

(If you would like to complete an on-line assessment and receive a personalized report which will help you discover your Driving Forces simply go to www.kabachnick.com

Here are the six Values that determine your Driving Forces and how they affect your behavior:

- **Theoretical**: One's passions to discover, analyze, and know. A search for knowledge. A need to learn.
- **Utilitarian**: A passion to gain a return on investment of time, resources, and money. Time is money. A drive to be practical.
- **Aesthetic**: A passion to add balance and harmony in one's life and protect our natural resources.
- **Social**: A passion to eliminate hate and conflict in the world. A need to help and assist others.
- **Individualistic**: A passion to achieve position and to use that position to influence others. A need to control one's destiny and the destiny of others.
- **Traditional**: A passion to pursue the higher meaning in life through a defined system of living. A need to live by a defined rulebook.

How do you determine Values or Driving Forces without an assessment?

Understanding someone's Driving Forces is critical to the relationships that you create and maintain with people. Most disagreements occur because our Driving Forces differ from the individual we are trying to understand. This brings to mind a recent situation between two long-time friends.

Linda and Susan are driving down a road in downtown St. Petersburg, FL. These two are friends whose communication styles are so similar that many times they don't even have to say anything—they just look at each other and finish each other's sentences. They're totally in sync. As they're driving they're laughing and talking about a recent party they went to—expressing similarities in their observations of the people at the party. They then come across several obviously homeless people on the sidewalk. All of a sudden Linda turns to Susan and says; "Geez I wish these people would just get a job and stop being so helpless and expecting others to support them". Susan is upset at what Linda just said and says to Linda; "How can you say that? You have no idea what caused this person to be in the situation they're in." In a very short period of time these two close friends are in a heated discussion—neither willing to concede to the other's point of view. Will they ever change their minds and see things from the other perspective? No they won't. Their Driving Forces differ greatly.

Linda's top significant Driving Force is Utilitarian—she is practical and believes strongly in investing time and money to bring about a return on that investment. Susan however has a very high Social Driving Force. She wants to eliminate hate and conflict in the world and bring about a world where people help each other. I call this the Mother Teresa value. Regardless of their companionship and twin like communication patterns Susan and Linda differ greatly. Values and Driving Forces differences bring about more conflict than behavior differences because they are driven by emotional reactions to situations. Communication patterns and preferences can be adapted to situations. Driving Forces are difficult to adjust or adapt because they are at the core of what we believe and why we do what we do.

You can discover someone's Values or Driving Forces by paying attention to the person. It basically is as simple as that. But we don't pay enough attention to others because we don't know how to ask questions and then listen. As an example, let's look at a typical Monday morning encounter between two co-workers:

"Hi! How was your weekend?" Answer: "Fine. How was yours?" Answer: "Was okay. No big deal." Both workers move on. Those wasted few seconds revealed nothing and it was a typical zero exchange that many of us experience.

Now let's change that exchange into one that will help us discover something about our co-worker that we don't know:

"Hi! How was your weekend?" Answer: "Fine." Comeback: "What did you do?" Answer: "I finally got a chance to go to the beach and read a book." Comeback: "That sounds so relaxing. Do you enjoy reading?" Answer: "Oh yeah- I love to read. I just don't get a chance to do it often." Comeback: "Any particular books you enjoy?" Answer: "Just love all types of topics."

This exchange probably took all of one minute and look at how much you learned. This person has a very high Theoretical Value and has a passion for knowledge.

What could have been another insight?

- The person could have said they spent a day volunteering at a homeless shelter. Discovery: A high Social Value.
- They could have said they spent time analyzing their investments and catching up on their Barron's reports. Discovery: A high Utilitarian Value.
- They could have said they went to the latest Dali exhibit at the museum. Discovery: A high Aesthetic Value.

- They could have said that they keep a journal and try to recall their experiences from the past week and determine what they could improve on in the coming weeks so that they live up to their principles and help others to live a better life. Discovery: A high Traditional Value.
- The person went to the office to work on a project that would help her advance her promotion and also position her team as winners. Discovery: A high Individualistic Value.

Values/Driving Forces are invaluable in giving us an insight as to what drives a person and provides us with a GPS into forming a more substantial relationship.

Here's a questionnaire to help you determine your primary Values/ Driving Forces:

Theoretical Attitude Statements

Scoring Scale: 5=Always 4=Most of the time 3=Sometimes 2=Rarely 1=Never

(Circle One)

5 4 3 2 1   I greatly enjoy discovering, understanding and ordering knowledge.

5 4 3 2 1   The pursuit of knowledge, identifying truths and untruths motivates me.

5 4 3 2 1   I am good at integrating the past and present.

5 4 3 2 1   Many see me as intellectual.

5 4 3 2 1   People who make emotional arguments without the
              facts, frustrate me.

5 4 3 2 1   I have a keen interest in formulating theories and asking
              questions to assist in problem solving.

5 4 3 2 1   I am fulfilled by work that requires ongoing education
              as well as the use of my knowledge.

5 4 3 2 1   Every time I am near a bookstore, I want to stop in.

5 4 3 2 1   I use knowledge to convince others of my ideas and win
              arguments because of the facts I know.

5 4 3 2 1   I want to know just for the sake of knowing.

Let's assess your Utilitarian Attitude. Here again are ten statements
that you will need to circle a 5 – 1 response based on how well the
statement describes you. Remember, there is no right or wrong answer.

Utilitarian Attitude Statements

Scoring Scale: 5=Always 4=Most of the time 3=Sometimes 2=Rarely
1=Never

(Circle One)

5 4 3 2 1   I evaluate things based on their utility and economic
              return.

5 4 3 2 1   I tend to move to practicality in all areas of life.

5 4 3 2 1   I am very conscious of the use of my time, achieving
              the most for the minute.

5 4 3 2 1   I desire an adequate return on any investment I make.

5 4 3 2 1   Wealth provides the needed security for my family and myself.

5 4 3 2 1   I am very future oriented.

5 4 3 2 1   Money and possessions are scorecards of my success.

5 4 3 2 1   I want to be rewarded accordingly for my time and effort.

5 4 3 2 1   I attempt to structure and control any economic dealings I have.

5 4 3 2 1   I tend to purchase things that have an investment value.

Always keep in mind that the six attitudes I am describing are not right or wrong. They have no morality. They are your way of viewing the world, the passions that move you into action. Here's an opportunity to assess your Aesthetic Attitude.

Aesthetic Attitude Statements

Scoring Scale: 5=Always 4=Most of the time 3=Sometimes 2=Rarely 1=Never

(Circle one)

5 4 3 2 1   I desire and seek the finer things in life.

5 4 3 2 1   I am in a continual self-improvement process.

5 4 3 2 1   I am aware of and enjoy the beauty of my surroundings and like my surroundings to complement my feelings.

5 4 3 2 1   I am very aware of my inner feelings.

5 4 3 2 1   I have a strong interest in the preservation of our natural resources.

5 4 3 2 1   Looking and feeling good is one of my goals.

5 4 3 2 1   I want harmony and balance in my life.

5 4 3 2 1   I invest time and money in self-help material.

5 4 3 2 1   I am very creative.

5 4 3 2 1   I look for and appreciate the beauty in things and in people.

In order to assess your Social Attitude, please read each of the ten statements below and circle a 5 – 1 response, based on how well the Social statement describes you.

Social Attitude Statements

Scoring Scale: 5=Always 4=Most of the time 3=Sometimes 2=Rarely 1=Never

(Circle one)

5 4 3 2 1   Eliminating hate and conflict in the world is one of my passions.

5 4 3 2 1   I have a passion to improve the whole of society.

5 4 3 2 1   I am generous with my time, talents and resources when I see someone in need.

5 4 3 2 1   I am empathetic to those who are hurting.

5 4 3 2 1   In business I will sacrifice bottom line profit for a more people-oriented decision.

5 4 3 2 1   I tend to avoid confrontation if it will harm the relationship.

5 4 3 2 1   I believe people should support charities.

5 4 3 2 1   In business I want everyone to receive the most that their money can buy.

5 4 3 2 1   Saying "no" to other is difficult when people need my time and talents.

5 4 3 2 1   I blame the system more than the individual and work to change the system.

Below are ten statements reflecting the Traditional Attitude. Please circle a number from 5 – 1 based on how well the statement describes you.

Traditional Attitude Statements

Scoring Scale: 5=Always 4=Most of the time 3=Sometimes 2=Rarely 1=Never

(Circle one)

5 4 3 2 1   I have a system for living and want others to follow my system.

5 4 3 2 1   Rules and regulations should be adhered to.

5 4 3 2 1   I tend to support organizations that hold the same beliefs I do.

5 4 3 2 1   I can be overly rigid in evaluating others against my standards.

5 4 3 2 1   I will be more helpful to others who share my beliefs.

5 4 3 2 1   My conscience is my guide.

5 4 3 2 1   I place a high value on living in tune with a higher purpose.

5 4 3 2 1   I believe my system for living is right and when challenged I will attempt to "convert" the person to my system.

5 4 3 2 1   I have found the "rulebook" for life and I follow it.

5 4 3 2 1   If I believe strongly in a cause, I will champion it.

Let's take a look at your Individualistic Attitude in the following ten statements below. Circle a 5 – 1 response that best represents your position.

Individualistic Attitude Statements

Scoring Scale: 5=Always 4=Most of the time 3=Sometimes 2-Rarely 1=Never

(Circle one)

5 4 3 2 1   I like people who are determined and competitive.

5 4 3 2 1   I believe that when the going gets touch, the tough get going.

5 4 3 2 1   It is important for me to be in control of my own destiny.

5 4 3 2 1   I strive to maintain my individuality.

5 4 3 2 1   I believe I can direct the destiny of others.

5 4 3 2 1   I want to be recognized for my accomplishments.

5 4 3 2 1   I believe if at first you don't succeed, try again.

5 4 3 2 1   I will work long and hard to achieve the position and influence I want.

5 4 3 2 1   I tend to believe "The end justifies the means."

5 4 3 2 1   I tend to play whatever "cards" necessary to gain control over the situation.

After completing the questionnaires on each of the six Values you have discovered which of these are your strongest—just average—or your weak ones. Now add up your scores and write that score in the space below:

_____Theoretical

_____Utilitarian

_____Aesthetic

_____Social

_____Traditional

_____Individualistic

The closer the number is to 50, the stronger that Value is for you. Which are your 2 top scores? Those then represent your most dominant Values/Driving Forces. If these are aligned with the job that you do, and where you do it you will "own what you do and love it too!" Otherwise you will feel a lack of fulfillment and passion and your work becomes just a job rather than an important life experience.

This questionnaire was developed and is owned by Bill Bonnstetter, Founder and Chairman of Target Training International. Many thanks to Bill for allowing me to use this powerful tool and introducing it to you. Let us know if you would enjoy seeing a comprehensive report of your Values and Driving Forces. Simply go to www.kabachnick.com.

OWN IT

- Be aware of your own Values/Driving Forces when making important decisions.
- Be conscious of trying to identify others' Values/Driving Forces when there appears to be conflict.
- Identify the primary Values/Driving forces that influence your company's culture.
- Ask some of the questions of your customers that you responded to, to help you better understand and serve your customers.
- Determine how aligned your Values/Driving Forces are with the role you serve or the role you hope to attain.
- What do you love doing?
- What are you best at doing?
- What do you believe is your strongest value to the organization?

"Enjoyment in what I do is more important to me than promotions. What I do is the contribution I want to make. It is my sense of achievement. I made that choice, and I am lucky because this company's standards are the same standards I was raised with—we share the same ethics. That's why I have been here for 30 years."
--Carol Brooks, Former Senior Manager, Education & Development Neiman Marcus

CHAPTER FIVE

Know Your Boss

Most people erroneously believe that it's the boss's job to pave the road for improved communication with their employees. This is misguided. The people who grow within their job learn to understand their boss's needs—whether they agree or disagree. Then they figure out a way to achieve their goals and convince the boss that their approach is the best for the boss and the company. An important element of achieving this is to recognize that communication plays an integral role. But you can't accomplish this by being illogical in your expectations of your boss. Since communication is a two-way street you can't leave it up to your boss alone to ensure strong communications—you must play your part. That means that sometimes you must initiate the communications and it also means that you must discern your boss's style of communication so that you both become fully engaged. Some people need all the information at once. Others want only the minimum facts and others want time to think about things before they come to any conclusions.

Think of it this way. What would you want your direct reports to provide you with if you were the boss—just the facts or all the details? Taking the time to understand your boss and her communication style will open your eyes to also understanding the people you work with— peers, team members, and customers. Before making a judgment look at things through your boss's eyes.

I live on a beach overlooking the Gulf of Mexico. One day I opened the doors to my balcony and heard weird noises. They sounded like chants or some type of mantras. These sounds kept repeating and getting louder. I stepped out onto the balcony and saw a group of people walking on the beach and they were making these sounds. I then saw dolphins in the water—which is not unusual—however I never saw them this close to the shore. Quickly I went down to the beach and ran over to the group of people chanting. I also saw more dolphins—about seven—swimming quite close. I asked one of the women in the group what they were doing. She told me they were talking to the dolphins—they were talking in the dolphins' language. The dolphins were responding by jumping up in the water and playing. I have never forgotten that experience and use it in my speeches and my coaching to emphasize the importance of understanding another person's preferred communication style.

Understanding how to effectively communicate is extremely important because much of your success depends on **who** you work for—more than **where** you work. Our research on successful people tells us that during the first three months of employment it is foremost on the new hire's mind to understand their boss—superseding even understanding what the new job requires. To some people this makes no sense but we've learned in our research folks who think like this don't get very far. For successful people the "getting to know you" period never ends.

Exit interviews and many surveys point to the fact that the number one reason people leave their jobs is because of their boss. This reason for leaving overrides compensation factors and lack of advancement opportunities. So, if you love what you do but do not like the person you work for is there something you can do? Short answer is YES.

Some people do not like the word "boss". They equate that title to a person who is domineering—authoritative—dictatorial—and of course bossy. Reality is different. All of us have bosses. Even if you're an entrepreneur you have a boss—most likely your banker or whoever is supporting your vision but wants to see results. So whether you are an individual contributor—a supervisor—a manager—a director— or an executive—you have a boss. Boss is not a negative title unless you think of it in those terms. Bosses should be viewed as leaders— mentors—coaches—and sponsors. Helping you be your own boss in controlling your work life is vital to your success.

Take a lesson from my dolphin story and ask yourself these questions:

- How much time have you spent getting to know your boss?
- Do you know what your boss is passionate about?
- Do you know her motivators? You may want to re-read the Values chapter.
- How does she speak to you? Is it similar or different from the way you speak?
- Do you observe your boss at work? Who does she spend time with? How does she spend her time?

- What are her hot buttons? What gets her upset?
- Do you watch how she conducts meetings? What can you learn from that observation?
- What does she demand of others?

See if this example resonates with you.

During a recent executive coaching session Mike, a Senior Vice President of Manufacturing sent out a cry for help to me. He was trying to understand Joan his boss. Mike asked; "Why can't I understand what she wants? The minute I seem to figure it out she changes something. I'm always second-guessing and I'm spending a great deal of time trying to figure out how to have the answers to the questions I know she'll be asking. Then when I'm all prepared she never asks me the questions—just listens to my brief update and tells me I've done a good job and to stay on the right track. Other times I'll be working on something and she'll walk into my office and ask me a question which she wants an immediate answer to, unrelated to what I'm working on. I get upset because I don't have the information right then and there. Mike said, "You have no idea how this frustrates me."

Mike – Mike – Mike I said, let me ask you a few questions.

Did you ever consider why when you're prepared Joan doesn't ask you questions? Mike thought about this for a while then asked back "Is it because I'm so prepared for the update that it comes across clear and decisive – I have confidence?" What do you think?

Mike, why do you get flustered when Joan asks you for something that you don't have an answer for right then and there? Mike quickly and simply said, "I feel I should have an answer. I feel like I'm disappointing her, that she'll see me as not on top of things."

Is this true? Would Joan think that of Mike? She might if he continues to react flustered, frustrated, and fumbling. However, what would happen if Mike took control and simply asked a question back. "Joan, do you need this information immediately or can I have two hours to get back to you? I want to make sure the answer I give you is right on. I'm currently working on this proposal for Adcliff, which needs to be finished for your approval by 1:00 pm." This approach does several things. First, Mike doesn't say "I don't know," plus he gives his boss the control of a decision. If Joan should say "I need this now," Mike could then ask if he can have an hour's extension to finish the Adcliff proposal.

I find that Mike and his frustrations are not unusual. If this happens at Mike's level in an organization, what happens at a less senior level of employment? The common problem is that employees (maybe even you) are afraid to ask their boss questions. But why? Why is the boss never questioned or asked for an explanation? Is it because the employee is afraid of the boss's reaction? Afraid they'll be perceived as "dumb"?

Now I'll turn this around and view the issue from the boss's perspective. What do I hear? Let's go back to Mike's boss Joan.

In my monthly debriefs about Mike's progress, I asked Joan about her interruptions and need to have answers from Mike immediately. She admitted yes it's true. If I'm working on something and need an answer, sure I'll go to Mike and see if he has it. If he doesn't have it right then and there he should tell me and then we'll agree to when I can get it. Joan's question to me was – look he's not a kid – why doesn't he speak up? I won't bite him! I asked Joan if Mike might be intimidated by her. Her answer was one I hear over and over from bosses. If I'm doing something to intimidate him he should have the b**** to have a conversation with me about this. I respect people who face a problem and discuss it—even if it's about me—even if it's about me.

There are many lessons to be learned from this but the most important is "get to know your boss quickly". How? Start by asking your boss for her "ticks me off" and "high expectations" list.

I share my lists with other bosses and encourage them to have theirs prepared so their new employee doesn't have to speculate. In the years I've been recommending this I've seen some truly outstanding lists and some hilarious ones.

An example of outstanding:

- Always admit a mistake—no matter how serious it may be.
- Never EVER lie to me.
- Be where you're supposed to be on time—preferably 5 minutes early.
- If you don't clearly understand what I want—ask me to explain.
- Stand up for what you believe.
- Stay home when you're sick.
- Lighten up!

Hilarious:

- Don't smell up your office with food.
- Don't say "God bless you" when I sneeze.
- Don't roll your eyes behind my back—I feel them.
- Don't tell me the latest joke you've heard.
- I'm not interested in who you kissed on the weekend.
- Don't patronize me—by saying things like "I understand your position".

When you invest time in understanding your boss and helping him achieve his goals he will provide you with opportunities to grow, he'll guide you and introduce you to people that will teach you. Many successful people who I coach inevitably refer to a former boss who was a beacon in their struggles to succeed—a person who took it to heart to help them achieve success.

Let's look at an example of success attributed to a boss.

Jim, was a struggling engineer for a manufacturing company in Silicon Valley where he had worked for seven years. His boss provided directives and more often than not negative feedback. As hard as he tried Jim could not get ahead with his boss. Jim had a family with two small children and felt that leaving his job was not an option. Besides, the economy back in 2008 was not suitable to even thinking of changing jobs. Jim felt he was glad to have a job.

In 2009 the company that Jim worked for was bought out and Jim got a new boss, Steve. The biggest surprise Jim got was when Steve asked Jim how he felt about his job. The second surprise came when Steve asked him what goals he had set both personally and professionally. Jim's previous boss had never asked these kinds of questions in all the seven years they had worked together. When I began working with Steve he asked me to dig deep into his key people and ironically, Jim was one of them.

Months later when I was working with Jim he told me about his initial meeting with Steve and the questions that Steve had asked him. He said that he was very embarrassed because all he did in response was to stare at his new boss.

When I met Jim he was full of doubt about his abilities—he was depressed and had no enjoyment in what he did. He also was not sure about what his future held. I asked Jim to complete an assessment that measured his competencies, behavior and work preferences, as well as his driving forces. I was quite surprised by the results because they pointed out a very skilled, competent, and determined individual. All these were within Jim however he never allowed himself to think about this or believe it. Working with Jim I coached him and provided specific homework and tasks for him to complete. It took a while to convince Jim that he really did have the potential to become a very successful person once he decided what he wanted to accomplish. He eventually decided that he wanted to become the Director of Engineering and then to work towards becoming a General Manager of a plant. What a pleasant surprise to see this person who thought so little of his abilities suddenly blossom and become strong in both self-confidence and in his vision.

In 2014 Jim became the Director of Engineering and is now working towards his goal of a General Manager.

Today Jim is very thankful to his boss Steve for providing him with the opportunities to discover himself and giving him the resources, like coaching, to guide him. I still work with Jim and am amazed at his continual growth.

NOW—A VERY IMPORTANT LEARNING POINT. What Jim learned was that he had to get to know Steve thoroughly. This meant he had to know Steve's goals, his objectives, his views on operating the business and his hot buttons. We decided that the best way to do this was for Jim to have informal meetings—like breakfast or lunch—with Steve on a regular basis. They did this twice a month. I recommended to Jim that during those meetings with Steve he should focus on "conversation" rather than numbers or strictly business related data. Jim learned how to ask questions and draw out Steve's ideas and thoughts. Based on what Jim learned he was able to focus his work on helping Steve achieve what he envisioned for his team and his operation. In doing this Jim experienced a win-win. He not only helped Steve accomplish his goals, Jim accomplished his as well.

OWN IT:

- Be the initiator in building a relationship with your boss.
- Don't be afraid to ask questions about your boss's vision—her needs—her expectations.
- Watch and observe—don't presume.
- Discover the pattern for communicating with your boss in the right way—both written and verbal.
- Anticipate problems and propose solutions.

- Let your boss know your expectations and goals. Bosses cannot read minds.
- Learn on your own. Don't wait for your boss to supply you with tools to get you ahead.
- Be enthusiastic about the company's products and/or services. Be sincere.
- Be positive even when things get difficult.
- Stretch yourself. What else can you do in addition to your given responsibilities.

CHAPTER SIX

Brand Yourself

If you were to leave your job tomorrow, would you be missed? If so, what would be missed about you? Your fun personality? Your friendship? Your ability to tell a good joke? Your depth of knowledge and contributions to create results? What would your colleagues and your boss say about you when you're gone?

It is critical to know what others think about you now, particularly those you work with and for. Do you know what your distinct qualities are? What makes you unique? Qualities are your attributes, your expertise, and your strengths. These are not necessarily your personality. Rather they talk more to your skills. Would you rather be known as someone who tells a good joke or someone who knows how to get people to see both sides of a conflict?

When you have a unique identity you stand out. Your name is on top of everyone's mind when they need something. Most everyone associates branding with multi-million dollar companies. When you need a search engine you use G*****. When you want to blow your nose you use a K******. When you want soup, you think of C*******. Even though dozens of products on the market do the same job, you still refer to certain products by their popular brand name. And yet most people rarely think of branding themselves. Even small entrepreneurial companies will try to brand themselves by developing a mission statement for what they want to do and accomplish. But rarely does that entrepreneur brand himself. Former CEO Bob Shaw did something unique to stand out years ago when he was applying for a job.

Many years ago Bob was applying for a top position at a company where he was vying against some formidable candidates. During his interview the executive asked Bob why he should choose him. Here's what Bob said:

"Let me explain it this way. A team of men are laying down railroad tracks when they hear the noise of an engine on the side track. The men look up and see an engine with a private car attached. A man leans out of the window of the private car and begins to wave. One of the rail workers waves back. The private car then pulls up alongside the workers and the man inside yells out, "Hey, Jim. Come on up."

Jim walks over to the private car and climbs in. Chagrined and astonished the workers wonder what's going on. One hour later Jim joins the work team and waves goodbye to the man in the private car. His co-workers ask, "Okay, what's the deal?" Jim replies, "Oh, that's Dave Anderson. He's the president of the railroad." One of the men asks, "How do you know him?" Jim explains, "Well, 20 years ago we started working for the railroad on the same day; went through the same training."

Jim's fellow workers then asked, "So, why is he president and you're here working with us."

Jim paused for a moment, and said, "He went to work for the railroad. I went to work for fifty cents an hour."

After telling the story Bob simply stated that like the man in the private car, he was there to do whatever it took to help the company succeed. He was there for the company, not just himself.

By the way—Bob got the job!

Why is this important to owning and loving what you do? Because it gives you a clear sense of why you do what you do. If you're not sure of why you are in the job you're in how can you possibly love what you do? When you're not motivated how can you be passionate? If you are not passionate how can you feel ownership? Motivation, as I tell managers and leaders worldwide, is nothing more than people knowing that they are making a difference – contributing to the success of the organization. I will repeat this because whether you are a contributor, a manager, an executive or an entrepreneur, knowing that what you're doing makes a difference is the distinction between you as a brand and you as just another worker. It impacts co-workers, the organization, and the bottom line results. Yet I find that few can answer these questions when I ask them. What are you known for in this company? What would others say about you? How do you stand out?

As my dear friend and colleague, Dr. Len Berry, Presidential Professor for Teaching Excellence and Distinguished Professor of Marketing and Professor of Humanities in Medicine at Texas A&M University says, "It's not what you say you are, it's what your customer says you are …" How true but you may say, "I don't have customers. I work in a lab." Oh, but yes you do. Everyone that you interact with is your customer. What do they say about you?

If you don't brand yourself, others will. So let's start at the beginning.

Why Did You Hire Me?

Why were you hired? What differentiated you from your competitors? What sold the hiring decision makers on you? Do you know? If you don't then you've already lost the competitive advantage you came in with. Because if you don't know, then you probably have not acted on or magnified the very reasons you were chosen. Was it your personality? Your experience? Your skill sets? Or a combination of all? All of these factors are at the very essence of creating your own unique brand in order to be differentiated, noticed, recognized, and ultimately rewarded.

To begin to understand the power of having a personal brand you first need to ask yourself these questions. Then compare your answers to what others say when you ask them:

- What's unique about me?
- What do others come to me about for help?
- Who do I naturally bond with and whom do I tense up with? (We tend to be most comfortable with people who are similar to us – so what traits do you see in those people?)
- What do I want others to say about me?
- What do I want to be known for?

Exercise: Ask some friends, family members, coworkers and others in your workplace who you interact with, but not on a daily basis, to give you three adjectives which they think describe you. Ask them to limit their answers to only three, as this is quite difficult for people to do. The natural tendency for most people is to make a list – and then you won't know which descriptors are really important. But when you ask for only three it becomes more difficult for people to choose the right words. Then take your time to review these. Is there a common descriptor that you notice? What is unique? A word perhaps coming from only one person? Do they describe how you act? Do they define your presence—your style—your attitude—or your being? You'll find that this exercise will give you a sense of empowerment and validation. Some things you may have already known. However, I find that most people who have done this exercise were somewhat pleasantly surprised at what they learned about themselves.

These questions and this exercise are not much different from what a company goes through when creating a brand that will be recognized, remembered, and talked about. The brand is a label—good or bad—that others give us.

You will need to focus on where you want to go—the people you want to influence—the lasting impression you want to make on others—in order to begin building your brand. The best way to make a lasting impression is to help others achieve their goals. Step in and take charge when others cannot or will not. Please note: You don't need a title to do this. However, don't be the martyr or the do-gooder. These are not good labels. Simply solve the problem and then subtly let the people who matter know about your accomplishment.

Larry, who works for a technology company in California, used the above strategy to move up from a trade show representative and a copywriter to his current position of Marketing Coordinator. He let everyone he worked with know that he was always willing to help. He didn't talk about it he just did it. Telling people you can help and waiting for them to ask you or asking them if you can help is like asking someone how he feels. What's the answer 99% of the time?

This is not difficult—it simply requires awareness. Larry was observant, a good listener, and watchful. He didn't bury his head in his work totally oblivious to what was happening around him. He made it a point to walk around and chat. He told me he got this idea from reading about the management concept of MBWA – Managing By Walking Around. He figured if it was important enough for executives to do it would benefit him even though he wasn't even a manager.

So Larry walked—and listened—and observed. Just barely into his first month on the job Larry saw a coworker in customer service looking angry and annoyed. He went over to him and said "Hey Jim – what's up? You really look P.O.'d. Jim explained the problem he was having with a customer who was blaming him for a late order—2 weeks beyond ship date. When he went to the shipping department they blamed the lateness on production. This wasn't the first time. When he went to production they blamed the delay on quality control. Jim told Larry that the customer was threatening to call the president of the company. Larry asked Jim what he thought the real problem was and Jim said he believed it was the lack of communication and standards for timing between the sales department and production. Larry asked Jim if he ever sat down with all the department heads involved and discussed these issues. The answer was no.

Larry suggested a meeting with a clear cut agenda to help resolve these issues and offered to be the facilitator since he was not involved. The meeting was held and the results changed the interaction between the departments—helping everyone understand the impact of one department on the other. The problem order was expedited and future work patterns greatly improved.

During the next debrief with his boss Larry mentioned the issues and suggested a company wide internal ad campaign that would focus on an "internal and external customer satisfaction" theme. Larry did not talk about his role in resolving the problems. But his boss asked how he learned about these issues and Larry briefly explained. His boss later discovered the important role that Larry played. Without saying much to Larry his boss told the company president about the incident. The president found out that indirectly Larry had saved an important customer.

Word spread throughout the company and Larry became the "go to" person. Nine months into his job Larry was promoted to Director of Marketing. Has he stopped being completely engaged? "No way," Larry tells me. His eye is now on a Vice President position.

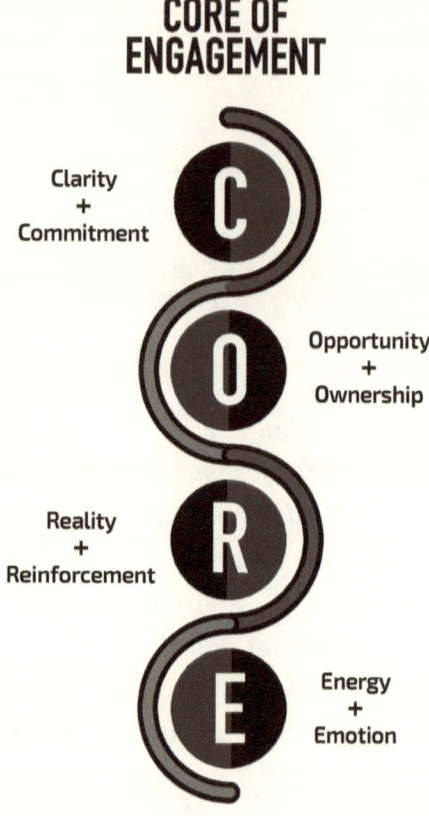

CORE OF ENGAGEMENT

Clarity
+
Commitment

Opportunity
+
Ownership

Reality
+
Reinforcement

Energy
+
Emotion

Think of your brand as a "mark." People who love what they do leave an imprint—sometimes unintentionally. I call it an imprint or a mark rather than a legacy because legacy is something the average Joe doesn't relate to. But if the average Joe loves what he does then he will leave an imprint—a mark. And the CEO of a major corporation will also leave an imprint. The marks we leave may be good or bad—large or small. These marks will be imprinted on those whose lives we touch—work with—live with—play with. What kind of mark will you leave? What will you be known and remembered for? What is or will be your brand?

Love your job and own what you do and the imprint you leave will touch many. Dislike or hate what you do and you also will leave an imprint.

At the Publix grocery store where I shop I always try to go to the checkout lane of Ben. He's friendly, engaged, and obviously loves his job. How do I know? When I buy eggs, he takes the initiative to open the egg carton and check all the eggs telling me he wants to be sure none are broken. He always asks if there's anything I've forgotten and if so, he is happy to go get it for me. And one day when I was buying a bag of pre-cut fresh vegetables he noticed that the expiration date was that very day. "When do you plan to use these," he asked? "If you aren't going to use them today, we'd better get you another one with a later expiration." Ben's just an ordinary guy doing an ordinary job, but because he loves what he does, he stands out from all the rest and as a result, I always shop at Publix and I always look for Ben.

OWN IT:

- It's important for your motivation and job happiness to know what others think about you—so ask. Use the three adjectives exercise as an easy way to accomplish this. Plus, it's fun to do.
- Learn from Larry. Reach out to others. Help them to solve their problems and achieve their goals. Yes, you do have time to do this. After all, how much time do you spend on the Internet?
- What do you do that is uniquely you—what's your distinction? Do others see this as unique to you? Remember, your brand is not your job title. Your brand is what others say about you. And what others say, sticks!

CHAPTER SEVEN

Control It to Own It

Control over one's immediate environment is a motivator and a prime reason for engagement. Lack of control represents loss of freedom. Loss of freedom feels like punishment.

One of our most cherished needs is to have a certain amount of control over our lives. This desire for control represents our freedoms. These freedoms can be large, like deciding where we want to live, or small, like deciding what we want to watch on TV. Freedoms are the choices we make everyday. These choices enable us to have good feelings. Some examples are, being in charge, having power, controlling our destiny, feeling smart, and a host of others. However, this ability to control—to have freedom—to make choices—to have ownership—is sadly lacking in the workplace for many people.

In the past twelve years, The Kabachnick Group has surveyed many companies and organizations and hundreds of workers using our employee engagement assessments. We have found that the highest level of dissatisfaction among all ranks of employees came from areas that addressed decision-making, control over work, and control of time. When asked the following questions 72% of employees either disagreed or strongly disagreed.

- I am satisfied with my level of involvement regarding the decisions that affect my work.
- I am able to make changes in areas of my responsibilities without asking for permission.
- I am able to allocate my time as I see necessary in order to get my job done.
- I feel in control of my time and my work.
- I am encouraged to make changes in procedures and processes in order to improve workflow.

These five areas of work therefore are extremely important to determining your level of happiness in the work you do.

Outside of work we also expect a certain amount of control. We feel empowered and responsible to make our own decisions. We have choices. But at work we often don't seem to have much control. For example, you may handle a customer complaint and feel you did a really good job. After all, the customer praised your efforts and thanked you. However, your boss disagrees with how you handled the situation and tells you that next time you need to ask him before "you give the store away." Given this situation most people would simply accept the boss's comment, walk away, feel dejected, and probably not be so responsive to the next customer's complaints.

Bosses respect people who think and speak up when they disagree. What could you do to leverage some personal control?

First of all, learn to speak up by asking questions when you don't agree with a boss's evaluation or perception of a situation. Contributors, managers, and executives at all levels generally accept a boss's statements as dogma. But whoever said that a boss is right just because she's a boss?

I know what you're thinking! I'll say it out loud; "You don't know my boss." Oh yes I do. You see I coach many of these bosses—the ones who not only think they're right but outright tell you they're right and you're wrong. And yet these very same bosses ask me, "Why don't more of my people speak up when they disagree with me? Why are they afraid? They're big shots when they face their peers, their customers and their competitors. Yet put them in front of me and they act like little kids in front of Daddy." This is an actual quote. I could share more insights but I think I've made my point.

> *At a large IT company based in California, a Senior Executive whom I'll refer to as Mark, was criticized and verbally beaten up by his boss, Dave, the President of the company. Dave thought Mark wasn't paying attention to the way his directors were managing a large facility's expansion project. In Dave's mind, after visiting the site and speaking to some directors, he was frustrated and upset so he walked away with what he thought was their casual approach to the work, and lack of seriousness, as represented by a "don't-worry-we've-got-it-under-control" attitude. Dave told Mark in no uncertain terms; "If you don't step in and corral these idiots and give them clear marching orders then I'll do it. They don't understand we've got deadlines and budgets to meet. They're acting like they're building a home extension in their spare time."*

Had this "conversation" with Dave occurred a year earlier Mark would have agreed and gone to his directors and read them the riot act. He would have gotten physically involved in the work and showed his boss that he was a good soldier. However, Mark's new approach in managing his directors was a result of the coaching he received from me. He learned that in order for his directors to own their jobs, be engaged in their actions, and really love and be proud of their work he had to allow them to make decisions that he had made for them in the past. Instead, Mark now held regular meetings, created an atmosphere of "nothing but the truth," and resisted his natural tendency to micromanage every detail of the project. Because of Mark's new initiatives the project was ahead of schedule and on budget. He had fewer people problems than in the past and his "guys" were working as a team. Obviously this attitude was foreign to his boss. As a result Mark's response to Dave's comments was also different. Instead of immediately following Dave's demands, Mark asked Dave if he could grab a few things and meet with him in about ten minutes so he could better understand Dave's concerns. Dave willingly agreed. Mark owned it.

OWN IT:

* *Always allow a person a few minutes to decompress before continuing a contentious conversation.*

Mark began by asking questions.

"Dave, I appreciate your concerns and would like to have more input as to what you found during your visit. Can you give me some more details?"

Dave: If you were there instead of sitting in your office you would
　　　　know what's going on.

Mark: I was actually there a few hours before you and so I want to
　　　　see what you saw through your eyes.

Dave: You didn't see the lackadaisical and carefree attitudes?

Mark: There is a different attitude. And it's what I've been working
　　　　hard to encourage. I want an engaged and proud team that
　　　　accomplishes things through hard work but a team that also
　　　　works with pride and teamwork. Dave, I'd like to show you the
　　　　latest reports on the progress of this project. As you see we're
　　　　way ahead of schedule and we're even slightly below budget.

Dave　[thinking]: Are you telling me I'm seeing something different?

Mark: Different yes—in a positive way. It's something different because
　　　　we've never focused on how people feel at work and what
　　　　motivates them. We've never really asked what people want out
　　　　of their jobs. I got a real jolt when we did a survey of all my
　　　　direct reports. That's when I realized that I had better change my
　　　　management style or I may be losing some great talent.

If you're a contributor rather than a manager you may see this
example as irrelevant to your position. Don't dismiss this. Think big—
think beyond your job. Understand that if these types of situations
are taking place at this high level of a company with huge decisions at
stake (and these are high level people who don't have control over big
projects) what lesson may you learn from this? How might you apply
these lessons to what you do? How much easier may it be to control
smaller decisions with smaller risks?

Let's go back to the customer service incident mentioned earlier.
Knowing what you now know how would you have handled the

situation if you were the one who was criticized? Would you have walked away? Or would you have taken a few minutes, formed some questions to ask your boss, and then asked them?

To determine how you feel about the level of control you have in your job think about how you would answer these same survey questions asked above by choosing:

Strongly Agree – Agree – Somewhat Agree – Somewhat Disagree – Disagree – Strongly Disagree

- I am satisfied with my level of involvement regarding the decisions that affect my work.
- I am able to make changes in areas of my responsibilities without asking for permission.
- I am able to allocate my time as I see necessary in order to get my job done.
- I feel in control of my time and my work.
- I am encouraged to make changes in procedures and processes in order to improve workflow.

OWN IT:

- Think beyond what you do and think about what changes you can make to control more of what you do.
- What responsibilities are you good at and would like to do that you are not responsible for now?

When you are willing to make changes you will enhance your ability to be more in control, so let's see how you deal with change.

CHAPTER EIGHT

Own It to Love It

If you are in a job that you are not happy with I need to ask you a few very important questions:

- What role do you play in your unhappiness?
- Is there something you could have done differently before you accepted the job?
- Is there something you can do now? Or is it all someone else's fault?

Here is a partial list of what I call "blameitis"—a list that allows one to blame someone or something else for being unhappy. Blameitis is a pervasive illness that infects people at all levels in an organization who do not love what they do. As a result they blame: The boss – company policies – coworkers – direct reports – the economy – their salary – other people's salaries – the hours – the government – the industry – the lottery – their computer – their desk – their office – the insurance – the benefits – the travel or lack of – the customers—and on it goes. Do any of these possibly hit home for you?

All too often as an adult I hear from employees what I frequently heard as a child. I admit, I've even said it from time to time myself. "She made me do it!" It's a response that I thought excused me from being held accountable for my bad decisions. I remember my parents responding to me by saying (as yours likely did too) 'If she told you to jump off a bridge, would you do it too?" I have to admit, that was a good comeback. The lesson to be learned from my parent's response is, we all make choices and once we make a choice, we have to own it! If you are in a job that makes you unhappy, you made some early choices that put you there. You applied for the position, you went for the interview, and you ultimately accepted the job.

Things don't always work out the way we think they will—but you always have choices. If you don't love what you do now, you can make another choice. You can choose to leave or you can choose to stay. If you have already decided to leave then quickly jump to the last chapter in this book. However, you also might benefit from examining some of the ideas, suggestions, and tips I provide in the upcoming chapters.

If you want to stay and learn how to love what you do then you have to go to work for yourself. Yes—you read that right. When you work for yourself there's no one to blame but you. Passion for doing what you do begins with job ownership—job ownership begins with owning your inner self.

Whether your choice is to leave or stay in your current job, I believe you'll find value in the following:

I use this lesson as the foundation of my coaching and consulting. I emphasize that before you can grow and change you must have—or you must develop—ownership of five important tenets.

1. **Own your thoughts.** How you think will determine what you believe and influence how you act.
2. **Own your beliefs.** Believe in yourself; believe that you do your best and your best is good enough.
3. **Own your words.** Say only what you truly mean.
4. **Own your actions.** Behave in a way that you would be proud of should a video of you show up on You Tube.
5. **Own your responses.** You have a choice in how you respond and react to any situation—unexpected or not.

Following are examples for each of the five tenets:

Own Your Thoughts

Melissa is a 32-year old Administrative Assistant to the Senior Vice President of Global Sales for a company that produces plastic molds. She's been in her job for almost four years. Recently Melissa started thinking that people were taking advantage of her good nature and willingness to help out in all situations. She thinks that because it's hard for her to say "No" and refuse to help, she has become a magnet for attracting tasks that have nothing to do with her job responsibilities. Rather than address this issue with her boss or a close associate Melissa has kept these thoughts to herself. Eventually she began to see the situation not as a perception, but as a reality.

She began to believe that she had become a "doormat"—her words. Melissa's beliefs began to affect her behavior and how she responded to others. Inevitably others noticed her changed demeanor and an uncharacteristic negative attitude. Thankfully her boss was perceptive enough to notice her changes and addressed them. Melissa learned that she alone was responsible for how she thought about situations, people, her job, and herself. In the end it doesn't matter what others do or say. How you think will be how you act. When you fail to own your thoughts and your resulting beliefs you simply become a victim.

OWN IT: *What you think is what you say and eventually what you will believe.*

Own Your Beliefs

Many wrong decisions and poorly calculated risks are a result of ego and one's need to be seen as powerful and accepted.

S. Truett Cathy, the founder of Chick-fil-A had a strong belief and passion for family values. He believed in families spending time together—especially on Sundays when all family members were usually at home together. When Cathy opened the first Chick-fil-A he decided that the restaurant would be closed on Sundays so his employees could be home with their families. For this decision he was openly criticized by many business people who questioned how a fast food restaurant could survive being closed on one of the highest volume days of the week. Staunch in his belief that he was doing the right thing, Cathy never gave up. Today, Chick-fil-A surpasses McDonald's in per store sales. On average, McDonald's annual per store sales are $2.5 million while Chick-fil-A's are $3.1 million and Chick-fil-A does this while operating only six days per week.

***OWN IT**: Have you gone along with ideas or decisions that you instinctively know are wrong or won't work just because of your ego or because you want to belong or be accepted? Do you second-guess yourself rather than confidently believe in yourself?*

Own Your Words

Josh is a 46-year old Vice President of Operations at a non-profit organization. He is considered by many to be a great communicator and is always called upon to speak to organizations to raise money. Josh has become so comfortable in his role as a spokesperson that often he simply doesn't think about what he will say. According to Josh " ...the words will be there when I need them." After one of his impromptu speeches Josh was criticized by one of the large contributors who said that Josh misspoke when he told a group of supporters that, " ...even though the economy is bad and everyone is cutting back I know you guys always have some hidden funds available to you whenever you need them for a pet project ..." Contributions declined noticeably after Josh's speech. Word soon spread throughout the organization about his cavalier comments. Instead of owning the problem, Josh blamed it on a misunderstanding. The reality was it was his choice of words that derailed Josh. He simply refused to own his words—words that were of his choosing

OWN IT: Words are powerful; that can be good and it can be bad. Have you possibly created or added to your unhappy situation because of something inappropriate or hurtful you may have said in a moment of stress, then later regretted it?

Own Your Actions

Your actions are a result of the above 3 tenets—your thoughts—your beliefs—your words. What you think about, what you believe, and how you speak will result in how you act. This is especially true during stressful times when your subconscious will often override your conscious decisions to act in an appropriate manner. For instance, if you dislike someone your thoughts about that person will be unconstructive. Your beliefs about him will be pessimistic. And your words may be abrupt and not always kind. So if that individual comes to you with a problem or criticism and happens to catch you at a bad time, your immediate [subconscious] response—your actions—will be negative even though your conscious mind is telling you to act differently.

OWN IT: Always be conscious of your negative thoughts, your beliefs, and your words. Insist on finding something positive about a person, a situation, or a challenge. Your subconscious acts like a hard drive and stores your experiences similar to how your computer saves information. If you save negative feelings and emotions you will react negatively. Program yourself so you can count on positive actions as your default program—a natural response.

Own Your Responses

How you respond and when you respond sends a powerful message to others. It's all about self-management and self-control. Many people feel that when asked for an answer they must provide one. Just look at the etiquette of email—or lack of. When you send an email how quickly do you expect a response?

In a recent survey of over 600 employees in a tech company 82 percent of respondents stated that they expected a reply to their emails by at least the end of the business day when the email was sent. In another question, when asked how quickly they responded to emails 76 percent said that their response time was determined first by who sent the email. The higher up in the company hierarchy the quicker the response. Considered next was how important the subject of the email was to the recipient. Most of the respondents agreed, however, that responding quickly was something they felt they had to do— even when they had more important things to accomplish and even when they lacked the information for a correct response.

What's wrong with this picture?

OWN IT: What is your response pattern? Do you feel you have to respond to every inquiry or question? Have there been occasions where you were talked into responding to an idea in a way that seemed logical, but in your gut you knew something was wrong? Do not respond when you are in doubt. Or if you are not sure what the correct response should be. When you are pressured for a response, saying "I don't know" is much better than giving a response you either don't believe in or are not factually sure of. Unless you are in a life and death situation where an immediate response is mandatory you always have time to formulate a good response. Never allow anyone else—even your boss—to force an answer that you don't believe is accurate.

Now apply these tenets to yourself. Ask yourself, before you made a decision on the job you're in, did you really take ownership?

Own and Improve

Think of owning your job in the way you would own a house. When you own a house, be it a new one or one you've owned for a while, there's always room for improvement. You can improve your house in four ways:

You can REFURBISH— RENEW—REMODEL ––or REPLACE. Now think of your job in these same terms. If the passion is gone and you don't love what you do you can:

REFURBISH your job. You have decided you don't want to change jobs—you just want to restore it to what it was when you first started. You were excited, motivated, engaged, and happy. Now the sparkle and shine is gone. It's become boring. You loved learning and growing but somewhere you took a detour and now things are dull. What areas need a new coat of paint? What needs a good cleaning? Where are the cobwebs and what's gotten moldy and unclear?

For example, what is it you're really accountable for? Do you even remember what responsibilities are in your job description? Could it be time to renegotiate/refurbish your job description?

RENEW your job. You are noticing that some things are cracked or broken— Relationships?—Communication?—Responsibilities?—Feedback? Due to lack of attention things are now in need of repair. Start by tackling the big cracks first. When the big cracks get fixed many times the less obvious ones seem to go away. Is it a co-worker you no longer have time for? Is the communication with your boss now limited to only job related topics? Are you no longer invited for a "let's grab lunch" get together?

If you're no longer being invited for lunch, take charge and do the inviting. If communication with your boss is limited, initiate the talks. In other words, be proactive and renew what you are missing.

REMODEL your job. You need more space. You are getting frustrated with the framework of your job—which has changed in responsibilities but not in other areas such as decision making or budget control. You may need more help but can't get the okay. Here's where you need to set priorities just as you would if you were remodeling a house and had a limited budget. What's more important; a new deck with a pool or a new kitchen? Where will the biggest return on investment be? The return on investment in this case is you. In what area of your job can you show growth and improvement to prove the investment in you will be worthwhile?

REPLACE your job. If you have tried refurbishing – renewing – and/ or remodeling but you've just outgrown the house or the house no longer meets your needs it's time to find something new. However, don't make this decision lightly and never make it when the emotional part of your brain is controlling the logical part. Take your time. Listen to your inner voice—your subconscious. Use the "Must Do" formula below and if the decision to leave comes up as the answer then read the last chapter in this book.

Own It Exercise: Your job is one of the most important areas of your life. It affects your health, your happiness, and most aspects of your life. Just like you take care of your body by going to see a doctor annually for a physical [You do don't you?] you must take the time to do a "physical" on your job every year. Take the time to go somewhere that you find peaceful. Go alone. This could be a beach or another place near water, a forest, a park, or a mountain— wherever you feel the most relaxed. Plan on two to three hours of time. Bring a pad of paper and a pen. No laptop or other electronic device allowed! The reason is that your brain works in a different way when you're writing versus typing. Writing has a greater impact of embedding your thoughts on your brain, thus making the ideas more realistic, possible and attainable.

When you arrive at your destination take a few minutes and absorb the atmosphere. Ask yourself why these surroundings relax you—why do you enjoy being here? Then begin thinking of your job and start writing whatever comes to your mind. Don't edit—don't try to figure out why you're writing what you're writing—just write and you'll find yourself in a hectic pace to keep up with your thoughts and ideas. When your mind begins to stray—as it will—to areas other than your job—like what you have to remember to pick up at the supermarket—push your mind to stay focused on your job. Continue writing until you start feeling tired and your mind is almost blank. Take some time to refocus on your surroundings and drink in the beauty of where you are. Take a deep breath—relax! You've done a lot of work. After you get home put your notes away for 10 days. Do not read what you wrote.

After 10 days find some quiet time to review your notes. As you're reading what you wrote use a highlighter to call attention to the areas where you question what you wrote and why you wrote it. You will find yourself wondering what did I mean— why was I thinking about this? After you highlight these areas you'll reread them and you'll discover a repetitive pattern— something or someone related to your job will surface. At this point you'll realize there may be areas within your job that you want to focus on—maybe people you want to have stronger connections with—tasks you may want to eliminate or add— goals you may want to set for your next move. Doing this kind of "physical" on your job every year will help you decide which of the above "Rs" you want to focus on. Now you will be able to more confidently decide—Do I Refurbish, Renew, Remodel or Replace? The choice is yours.

When you become accountable and own the choices you make you not only become more valuable in the role you play, you also become more likely to be happy with the work you do which is the first step toward loving your job as well.

CHAPTER NINE

Danger in the Comfort Zone

Are you bored? Maybe you're just pretending to be comfortable in your job and fine doing what you're doing? After all, it's "just a job". If that's the case, consider this. Your boss and others may see your comfort as complacency, lack of interest or initiative, disengagement or mediocrity. So what do you think your next review will sound like? How long can you just exist? Not long in today's world. Today, everyone is expected to do more with less and you better than anyone, know it didn't start out this way.

A new job, like a new relationship, is initially quite exciting and stimulating. As time goes on there are peaks and valleys. The more time that passes the more the landscape evens out and becomes flat and boring creating stretches and stretches of same old, same old.

When you started your job did you make a list of all the things that you were going to change and improve? Did you have lots of ideas? Did you talk with others and run your ideas by them? Did you make suggestions to your boss? Then what happened? Things settled down and you slowly lost your excitement. Routine took over and the familiar became safe. So now you don't hate your job but you don't love it either. You have become part of a statistic. If you're an average worker, regardless of your position—contributor, manager, executive, or leader—boredom can set in before you're in your job one year. And then if everything else is okay—no mean boss for instance—you'll likely stay this way for another two years before you begin to start finding fault, getting upset at little things, and complaining to friends and family. The irony is, whose fault is all of this, really?

Loving what you do always means leaving your comfort zone—stretching yourself and discovering abilities you didn't know you had. How can you be passionate and be bored at the same time? It's impossible! Loving what you do and having passion for accomplishment will vary in degrees based on your behavior preferences. Some people love constant challenges. Others prefer working within a more stable environment. Regardless of where your comfort meter registers on a scale of one to ten—ten being constantly craving challenges and one having very few challenges—you need to step outside your comfort zone in order to stay engaged, motivated, and happy. It's a matter of degrees. But to own what you do and love it too you need to stretch, grow and step outside your comfort zone.

EXCITEMENT

GROWTH

COMFORT

COMPLACENCY

BOREDOM

DISENGAGEMENT

THE DANGER ZONE

The concept of pushing past your comfort zone may be difficult to understand because we don't want others to see our imperfections, lapses or flaws. We want to be stars. We want to be seen in the best light. Witness what happens when an actress, a star, is caught by the paparazzi without makeup and looking disheveled. Battles have been fought over less. And yet when we encounter someone who is genuine enough to expose their shortcomings, their inconsistencies and their imperfections—what is the result of this discovery? How do we feel? Over the years I've found that the answer is that people feel drawn closer to such a person—trusting them more than those who worry about being perfect.

Recently, at several different organizations' off site retreats for managers and executives, I experimented with an exercise that required the managers and executives I was working with to move past their comfort zones. The objective was to show each person what he or she could accomplish by stretching themselves, facing their fears and overcoming obstacles. To experience how they could become better decision makers, be more creative, and understand people better. The participants became rubber bands—pushing themselves to stretch as far as possible without breaking their elasticity. The assignment was quite simple—the results, however, were profound.

The Assignment

For this exercise, each person was asked to think about what they most feared doing, or what they could never imagine themselves doing, and then to go out and do it. Partnered with a buddy each had support to confront their fears and challenges. Partnering also ensured that they wouldn't chicken out. Here are some real examples of what they confronted and what they learned:

Dennis feared spiders to the point of passing out when he would merely see one at a distance. He would even begin sweating when he'd see a spider in a picture. To confront his fear, Dennis and his buddy went to a pet store. After some encouragement from his buddy Dennis allowed the pet store associate to put a tarantula spider on his arm. Dennis stood there barely breathing while the spider crawled on his arm for several minutes. Encouraged by the associate Dennis cautiously touched the tarantula and felt its velvety body. He later told the management team that the feeling he experienced at that point was unlike anything he had felt before in his life—a feeling of power and a sense that he could overcome anything or face any challenge. It was an incredible turning point for Dennis.

Patrick was so terrified of heights he could not visit certain places with his family, his buddies, or his team. Feeling left out on many occasions Patrick became withdrawn and depressed. Confronting this challenge seemed out of the question for him. However, when he realized that he was the only one in his management team to refuse to participate in team activities he had second thoughts. He knew that he would be embarrassed when it came time for the team debrief if he had nothing to contribute. Asking his buddy for every ounce of support he could muster, the two of them went to the Sears Tower in Chicago — now officially named the Willis Tower — where Patrick climbed hundreds of stairs. After finally reaching the top he stood at the windows and looked out on the panoramic view — then he passed out. Patrick's buddy, fearing that something like this might happen, had brought along some smelling salts. He administered them to Patrick who quickly came to. Bravely, Patrick once again stood and looked out from the 110th floor. Slowly he looked around, looked some more and then proudly gave an enormous shout and hugged his buddy and several other people nearby. Later Patrick became the star of the debriefing meeting. According to the CEO of the company, he has been a superstar ever since. Patrick's signature saying is now "on to new heights."

You can also use this exercise in a different way by asking yourself and others to share a mistake they have made and find out what they learned as a result. It is truly empowering not to have to be perfect in everything you do. Imagine starting a weekly staff meeting by asking everyone to share with others a mistake they made in the previous week and to explain what happened as a result of that mistake. Taking risks and accepting challenges keeps the fire burning; it keeps you being able to ask yourself, "Is there anything I can't do?" Sometimes we don't know our full capabilities and must push past our comfort zone to discover them. Start with the biggest fear; face it and all other fears will diminish or fade in comparison. Passions are fueled by that kind of fire.

In the process of leaving your comfort zone here are some things you might want to consider losing:

Lose the excuses – It's easy to not be accountable and blame others.

Ex: My research project is late because I didn't receive the data I needed from Marketing.

Lose the easy – It's easy to begin your day by reading your emails. Instead, what can you tackle that is new and outside of your comfort zone? And do it first thing in the morning.

Ex: Phil decided for three days out of the week to try not to begin his days by reading his emails—a daily habit. Instead he looked at the most difficult task he had on his "to-do" list for that day and started working on it, allowing himself a specific time frame before moving on to another task whether he finished the previous task or not. His sense of accomplishment was euphoric. He found that his energy for the rest of his day was incredible. Phil now uses his new found ritual five days a week. He also learned that by breaking down the big "to-dos" into smaller pieces he was able to get more accomplished which reduced his tendency to procrastinate the tough tasks.

Lose boring people – Comfort lies in sameness. It's easy to gravitate to those who don't push or stretch us. It's milk and cookies – comforting and relaxing. But what are you learning? How are you growing? Find those who challenge you, who push you; even those who may frustrate you.

Ex: Lori went to lunch twice each week with her work buddy Mary. She only did this because it's what she had always done, but she found that Mary always left her depressed and anxious. Lori decided to leave her comfort zone and told Mary that she couldn't have lunches with her that often anymore; she explained that she needed to make time for people in other departments of the company due to the projects she was working on. Then, despite the fact that she had previously avoided Jim, a manager from another department, Lori asked him to have lunch with her. She had avoided Jim because he was always challenging her in meetings but during her lunches with him Lori found that he was actually invigorating to be with and quite motivating in his enthusiasm over the projects he was working on. Eventually Jim told Lori that the reason for his challenges were to push her because he thought she was very smart and could be doing better. By Lori getting out of her comfort zone she developed a relationship with someone who had appeared to be a threat but actually turned out to be very helpful and also became a friend.

Lose your perceptions – It's easy to simply accept what you think is happening around you. It's easy to assume to know why certain people are who you think they are. Why certain routines are taken for granted. But it's much harder to question and ask for information as to the real why and how come.

Ex: We hear the saying "Perception is reality" quite often—and we believe this to be true. I beg to differ. I say: "Perception is reality only for the ignorant." A tough statement that always raises a few eyebrows. However, I believe that if you don't know the facts and you don't have the correct data then all you have are your perceptions—and most times they may be wrong and have nothing to do with reality. Whether it's what you think about the people you work with or the accepted ways of doing things within your organization if you don't know the truth then you will be wrong more times than right.

Lose the routine –What is the pattern that you work every day? What is your routine? What do you do when you arrive at work? What do you do before lunch—during lunch—after lunch? Do you feel secure having a routine? What happens when someone disrupts your routine—when something unexpected happens? Do you welcome the change in routine or do you resent it? Routines are treacherous. They force you into patterns that lead to low productivity and complacence. Break this pattern to move from your comfort zone.

Some examples:

- *Discover what someone is working on that for them may be proving difficult but you know that you are quite good at it. Perhaps it's a presentation they have to make and you are good at presentations. Offer to help them. This allows you to do something different and showcases a talent you may not be using all the time and that others may not know about you.*
- *You eat lunch at your desk and use this time to catch up on articles you need to read. Instead, ask someone to join you for a quick lunch and ask them about their most important to-do item. Share your most important item. Is there a way to help each other?*

- *Ask if you can be present at a meeting you normally would not attend. Rarely will someone ask you to be at a meeting that they feel may have no relevance for you. But that's exactly the point. Moving out of the comfort zone requires participation in areas you normally do not access. Imagine the insight you may get. Imagine if you give feedback from a different perspective—an unbiased viewpoint.*

Lose the pleasing – It can be very comfortable to just say "yes" in order to please and avoid conflict. It also gets quite comfortable to just do what someone asks you to do rather than offer a contradictory viewpoint—a point that you truly believe. If you slip into this pattern be assured your growth will stop and your reputation [your brand] will become that of "the people pleaser."

Ex: Emily is working on displays for a trade show booth and is ultimately accountable for the success of that booth bringing in new customers, generating traffic and ultimately resulting in plus business. A business development executive, a communication specialist, a representative from the PR firm, and also the President of the company, all have opinions on what she should be doing. Emily just wants to keep the peace and not confront. She agrees to what everyone offers as advice. Some of the ideas she implements, some she doesn't. The trade show does not produce the results expected. Whose fault is it? By trying to please everyone, Emily lost her focus, got off her main mission, and failed. All because it was easier to agree, stay comfortable and do what others asked rather than forget pleasing others and staying on the path she believed.

Comfort is easy. But what are the end results?

OWN IT:

- Ask yourself if you are focusing on tasks rather than results. Focusing on tasks is a sure sign of falling into the comfort [boredom] zone.

- What does loving what you do and having passion about what you do mean to you? Just you. Boredom and lack of passion conflict with loving what you do and most importantly, owning what you do. Decide what you want to move towards and what you want to move away from. You may want quiet passion—strong within you. Others may want prolific passion—visible to all. Passion is first internal before it becomes external. The flame burns deep within you. Once you have it, then you can control the degree of burn you decide to show externally.

CHAPTER TEN

Confronting and Conquering Conflict

In many of the surveys I've created, I ask "what is the biggest challenge you face within the workplace"? The most frequent response is confrontations or conflicts with others. When I asked for solutions to this challenge the answer was usually avoidance. Most people hate conflict, thus avoid having what I call "courageous conversations". As a result many things occur:

- Productivity suffers because people are preoccupied with emotions
- Gossip and perceptions take over reality
- Origin of conflict becomes distorted
- Small initial conflicts grow to larger conflicts
- Time spent on discussing conflicts averages eight hours in a week
- Trust diminishes and often is lost
- Good people leave

Here's a perfect example of how people often avoid confronting conflict:

> ### *Lunch in a Reston, Virginia restaurant.*
>
> *When traveling, I'll often try to find a restaurant within a busy business community, usually for lunch as that is when people gather and most often talk about their jobs. I love to take this time and catch up on my reading, reflect on my accomplishments, and also come up with ideas for my things to do—like my work on this book. Inevitably I'm drawn to and can't help overhearing the conversations around me. I love to listen especially when a person is complaining about their job or the people they work with.*
>
> *This was the case while having lunch at a busy Reston, Virginia restaurant. One person was complaining to his three coworkers about a department manager—Steve—who consistently was very defensive and would back up and support his people even when the mistakes they made were very evident. The person complaining said that Steve's actions hurt his team's output and morale. He said he couldn't take it anymore. One member of the foursome at the table spoke up and asked; "Tim, have you said anything to Steve about these issues?" Tim's answer was a simple "No". Silence at the table and then another question was asked; "Why haven't you?" Tim's answer was that he didn't want to make matters worse because he felt that Steve would blow up and he was afraid of that – plus he didn't know what he would do if that happened. The group agreed that Steve was a "ticking bomb" and that Tim should just try to work around Steve. Bad advice! I almost wanted to walk over to their table and share some insights and solutions. Obviously that would not be a good idea.*

The group left and I thought about how many times in my position as a trusted business advisor and coach I encountered situations where people simply wanted to avoid conflict at all costs. I then wondered how many times situations like this occur in companies and how often the solution to the problem is to do nothing.

To better understand conflict it is helpful to know the different types of conflict.

- Me/Me
- Me/You
- Me/Them

Me/Me conflict occurs within you. For example, should I make this decision or not. Should I proceed with what I believe is the right thing to do or not. If I ask for help would that be seen as my weakness. Constantly questioning yourself impacts your productivity and your strength in dealing with others.

Me/You conflict is mostly between two people and is usually personal and emotional. This can be a result of your perceptions about others based on your view of their gender – age – personality – and behaviors. How realistic are your views and have you sought facts that support your views?

Me/Them conflict focuses on teams – departments – groups – bosses. This is where you disagree on systems, procedures, goals, changes, and end results. These are the most difficult conflicts to deal with because you're combining the Me/You conflict with the Me/Them conflict.

How you approach resolving a conflict greatly depends on your natural proclivity towards conflict. Some people enjoy the challenge of a conflict and many times will actually seek out arguments and disagreements. They enjoy the battle. They love to fight. Their heart races and the adrenaline kicks in. They will strive hard to win these battles. Think Donald Trump.

However, most people—as I stated earlier—do not enjoy conflict and will go to great lengths to avoid it. Think Martin Luther King, Jr. This represents the majority of people in the workplace. Unfortunately this avoidance is costly both in the workplace and life in general. Go back to the beginning of this chapter and review the negative results I outlined when you decide to avoid conflict. They're not good!

Dancing around issues that create disagreements and often result in anger is unproductive and eventually creates a bigger problem. So learning how to have Courageous Conversations is vital to your success whether you are an individual contributor or a high ranking executive. Here are some tips to help you when conflict arises or has been an issue for a while. Step forward and address the issues. Doing nothing will eventually hurt your success.

Ten Tips for Conducting Courageous Conversations

1. **Check your ego—set your intention.** There's nothing wrong with a healthy ego, but your ego can get in the way of expressing yourself in ways that serve a positive outcome.

There's a difference between speaking up and talking down to someone—making them feel small, stupid or overly sensitive. Before you enter into a courageous conversation, be very clear in your mind about why you are having it.

2. **Mean what you say.** Be candid in your feedback and honest in your opinion. Say what you sincerely believe needs to be said, even if you know others may not enjoy hearing it. People can intuitively tell when you are being sincere. They can also tell when you aren't. Don't sugar coat the truth in fluffy compliments and disingenuous flattery.

3. **Set the emotional tone.** The more sensitive an issue, the more rapidly emotions can escalate to fever pitch when put on the table. If the issue you are addressing is likely to push emotional buttons, be extra careful to ensure you step into it calmly, with a clear idea of what you want to say. Remember, you have to manage your own emotions first before you can respond well to another's. If you start getting upset, call time out.

4. **Be vigilant of Victims and Villains.** As human beings we live in stories—about ourselves, about other people, and about the situations in which we find ourselves. The issue isn't that we have stories, but in believing that our stories are "the truth". Your stories can roadblock fruitful communication before you even begin. So before you engage in a tough conversation, think about the stories you are carrying into it—particularly any that cast yourself as a victim or others a villain. As in the storybooks, they tend to be fictional. Taking the time to genuinely listen to and understand another's story builds trust and makes others

more receptive to your opinions (growing your influence in the process). Listening to others' stories is the single most powerful communication tool you've got.

5. **Facts First.** There are always two sides to every story. Before you launch into your opinion of a situation, be sure to clearly state the facts as you see them. It's possible you may have incomplete information. When you present your opinion as though it is the truth, you are guaranteed to get people off side. Use language that leaves open the possibility of another interpretation on the situation. "I realize I may be missing something, but from what I can see it appears that ..."

6. **Discuss the 'Hush-hush'.** Issues that aren't talked out get acted out in snide remarks and innuendoes, higher absenteeism and turnover, and lower productivity and engagement. When you are discussing something sensitive, what is left unsaid is often what the conversation really needs to be about. Skirting around the real issue is fruitless. Likewise, burying your head in the sand in the vain hope that an issue will just 'go away' on its own is not only cowardly, it's costly. Acknowledge the unspoken; discuss the "hush-hush." The cost of engaging in difficult conversations far outweighs the discomfort you feel discussing it.

7. **Don't stoop.** People don't always act as we'd like or how we'd expect them to. Such is life. Don't let the bad behavior of others be an excuse for your own. While it's tempting to descend to the same level of pettiness or immaturity as others, it serves no positive purpose. Be the change you want to see in others—when they act small, act big.

8. **Counter defensiveness with humility.** When we share something with someone that has an implied criticism, we shouldn't be surprised when they get defensive. Counter their defensiveness by distinguishing the problem (behavior or issue) from the person. Invite their input in how to address the issue. Often the solution to a problem is far from obvious—to you or anyone else. Be willing to ask for help in figuring out a better path in order to move forward—acknowledging that you don't have the answer but would like to work together to find it. Just as you appreciate when others share their struggles openly with you, so too will others appreciate your candor and vulnerability.

9. **Be clear in your requests and commitments.** When going into a conversation, be clear about the actions or outcomes you'd like to see. Don't assume others know what you want them to do. Make clear requests with specific action plans.

10. **Stay future-focused.** There's a reason so many people excel at laying blame, throwing stones, and criticizing others' mistakes. It's easy. Staying focused on what needs to change to keep the same problem from arising again in the future takes more discipline. So regardless of how many stones you'd like to throw, let them go and focus instead on what you'd like to see more of—whether it's collaboration, clear communication, better systems, or more accountability.

Difficult People Versus Difficult Conversations

Knowing these facts will help you determine whether a courageous conversation will solve some of the issues you may be having with a person:

- Difficult people enjoy being difficult and they do it on purpose.
- They fully understand their behavior.
- In many cases their difficult behavior has been there for some time and may be the result of their low confidence and self-esteem.
- Their difficult behavior is directed at many people and it's not just directed at you.

When dealing with difficult people you have five choices:

- Do nothing.
- Understand the possible reasons for their behavior and then determine the consequences of having a courageous conversation.
- Consider what outcome would result.
- Adjust your behavior.
- Change your attitude.

OWN IT

- **Prepare** for your courageous conversation by understanding the other person's preferred communication style. Does he speak slowly and softly or is he quite direct and his conversation is delivered in a bullet format. Adjust your style to meet his.

- **Identify** the one most important reason for your courageous conversation. Do not attempt to cover more than one issue.
- **Obtain** as many specific examples as you can to support your reasons for this conversation.
- **Determine** the outcome you desire.
- **Focus** on an attitude of discovery and curiosity.
- **Present** the issue you are addressing in a few concise statements. Don't ramble or make excuses.
- **Refrain** from using the word YOU. Refer to the behavior you are looking to improve rather than the individual.
- **Create** a safe environment. Include in the beginning of the conversation the changes that you would like to see.
- **Ask** for the other person's input within the first five minutes of the conversation.
- **Listen** attentively—especially if you disagree.
- **Say:** "Can we start over?" if the other person begins to argue. Go back to the original reason for you having the courageous conversation.
- **Recap** the points of agreement and disagreement.
- **Repeat** the outcome that you would like to see and ask for agreement.
- **Get** agreement on timeframe.
- **Set** time for follow up and feedback.

Google chairman, Eric Schmidt, speaking at Boston University to the graduating class of 2012 said:

"I believe fully in the power of technology to change the world for the better. And I believe even more fully in the ability of your generation to use that power to great effect – to rule technology. But you can't let technology rule you … Take your eyes off the screen, and look into the eyes of the person you love. Have a conversation – a real conversation – with the friends who make you think, with the family who makes you laugh … Life is not lived in the glow of a monitor. Life is not a series of status updates. Life is not about your friend count. It's about the friends you can count on. Life is about who you love, how you live. It's about whom you travel through the world with. Your family, your collaborators, your friends."

CHAPTER ELEVEN

The Fear of Change

When I think about change, I can't help but be reminded of a quote from industrialist, John H. Patterson that so adeptly describes one's resistance or willingness to change: "Only fools and dead men don't change their minds." Could this be you? It could have been Bea, a woman who attended a workshop I conducted on change.

As I was beginning a workshop on change for a company in Baton Rouge, Louisiana, I noticed two women choosing a seat in the very back row of the room. The room was set up with long tables for approximately 80 people. It was quite crowded. About an hour into my session, I noticed the two women in the back row had their heads tilted down as if they were looking at something below the table. They didn't appear to be listening and weren't interacting with other participants. I decided to say something to them during the break.

When the break came, I walked over to one of them, introduced myself and went to shake her hand. That's when I noticed she was holding a book. I also noticed her nametag and with a smile I said; "I knew there was something that was holding your interest better than I was, Bea." Bea responded by saying; "Oh honey it's not you! It's just that I've been to so many of these types of workshops and I've learned that in the end, nothing really changes. But I have to be here so I try to make the best use of my time." Knowing that my workshops were different and actually did make a difference, I asked Bea if she would be willing to put away her book and give me her full attention until lunch. If after lunch she didn't feel she had learned anything new I would excuse her from the workshop and make sure her boss knew it was for a good reason. I had no clue what that reason might be – but I decided to take the risk. Bea agreed to do so.

During lunch, Bea came over and told me that she would be staying for the remainder of the workshop and would not be reading her book. I didn't get a chance to speak with Bea after the workshop but six weeks later, I receive a handwritten note in the mail. It was from Bea.

I was so humbled and touched to read that the workshop Bea so reluctantly participated in changed her life. She shared that after more than thirty years in a miserable marriage she went home from that workshop and "threw the bum out." Since then, she said her life had never been happier and she couldn't recall ever feeling more at peace. Bea wrote of her renewed passion in her job and how her sales continued to increase as a result. According to Bea, people seemed to notice the difference in her as well as she was frequently told how happy she looked. She ended her letter by verbally giving me the hug she said she should have given me on the day of my workshop.

Several years after receiving this note I got a call from Bea's friend [the one who sat next to her at the workshop]. She told me that Bea had passed after a short battle with cancer. She said she wanted me to know Bea had lived the happiest years of her life after attending that workshop.

Are you living the happiest years of your life? Do you have to make huge changes in order to do so? Are you willing to risk and change?

The workshop that I did so many years ago has evolved and grown. However, the basic principles remain the same:

1. The HOW in dealing with changes at work and in your life is the most important factor. Change happens to all of us all of the time. Some changes are made from necessity—your doctor tells you that you need to lose weight because your blood pressure is too high. Some changes are forced on us—your boss tells you that your office is being moved to make room for a new executive.

The HOW in dealing with change involves your mind-set and your beliefs about change. When you hear the word "change" do you immediately also see the word "big"? Most people envision any change as big. Think of *The Biggest Loser* television show. Can you imagine just naming the show *The Loser?* And herein lies the big reason why most people do not undertake change or maintain change for the long term—mentally they think it's a BIG undertaking. Thinking change has to be big is a fallacy.

2. Change usually occurs because it has to, not because you want to.

   - Must stop smoking because you can't take a deep breath
   - Must lose weight because the doctor scared you
   - Must work harder because people are being laid-off
   - Must work on a relationship because it's getting weaker

You rarely make changes when outcomes are positive. Changes are made when outcomes are negative. Do you remember the old saying: "If it ain't broke don't fix it?"

3. Resiliency and flexibility are the skills necessary to make changes when needed but they are also required when change implies improving rather than fixing. You should develop these two skills so you can change how you view your job and your responsibilities, which will then lead to how much you'll love what you do.

The best change—meaning sustainable and enduring change—occurs in increments—slowly. If you set out with a mindset that it has to be profound or "big" then failure follows. Why? Because just thinking about change causes fear.

I caution companies and bosses to try not to use the word "change." I use this example: When you say we have to "change" our commission structure, the first thing that happens is people become afraid, even angry. Fear sets in and the focus shifts from listening and trying to understand the new commission structure to focusing on "me." How will this affect me? What will happen to my pay? Why are they doing this to me? When you replace "change our commission structure" with "we will implement a new and improved commission structure" the focus becomes one of curiosity rather than fear. Semantics? Maybe. But words have a powerful impact on our emotions.

<u>Fear Factors</u>
F – Failure
E – Error
A - Abandonment
R – Reprisal

Fear of Failure

The change I'm attempting won't work and I'll be seen as a failure in the end. I'll lose respect. I'll be ridiculed. I may even be punished.

Fear of Errors

When I'm making changes I may make mistakes and end up looking foolish.

Fear of Abandonment

The familiar is better for me rather than the unknown even if it's detrimental to me right now. I fear being left behind or losing what I'm accustomed to—losing what has become a habit.

Fear of Reprisal

After I make changes, I'll be seen differently by others who may not appreciate these changes. I may no longer be a part of their lives. I may not be part of the old group. They may take revenge on me—they may be jealous of what I've accomplished. What if I'm promoted?

OWN IT:

- Small changes can bring big results. Think of one area in your job that you would like to change and write it down.

Example: *Kim wants to change because she's unhappy with her progress at work. She really wants to become an important part of the leadership team. She knows she's smart—knows she has the experience and insider knowledge of the company and its products. However, during meetings people talk over her. They take credit for her ideas—and she's nervous when presenting to a group. Kim expressed to me that she's tired of being this soft, wimpy thing and wants to have a strong persona.*

Follow these steps with Kim as an example of how you can ensure a sustainable change.

7 SECRET AND SUBTLE STEPS TO CHANGE

1. Question the real reasons and purpose for changing.

- What is behind your need to change? Is it because someone told you that you needed to change? Are you changing to be like someone else whom you admire?

- Is your reason for changing outer or inner driven? Success will only come if it's inner driven. You want to change because it will benefit you.

  Kim's example shows that she is inner driven and determined to achieve her goal of becoming a leader at her company. That's her passion!

2. Change your beliefs about change.

- Develop a statement that is your very own. Make sure it is in the first person and present tense. Frame it as if it has already happened. I call these your belief statements.

  Kim framed two belief statements:
  - *I am a valued team member respected for my ideas and how I present them.*
  - *I am a strong leader respected for my results.*

  By framing your belief statements in the present tense you will change your beliefs. When you change your beliefs you will change your actions. This will affect performance, engagement, your productivity, and love for what you do. Take ownership.

3. Don't tell anyone.

  Many change experts will tell you to seek support. They say that the more people who know what you are trying to accomplish the more who will support you. Well I differ with this rationale and here's why. Inevitably when you tell others about your change initiatives the focus will not necessarily be on you but rather on them. If these are coworkers, staff, or bosses their first thought will be—how will this affect me? Their main focus will be on how your change will affect them—first and foremost. This is a normal human reaction to any change. They will ask themselves what will happen if you accomplish this change. What will happen to how they do things? What will others think? People don't think about your benefits—they think about how your request for change will impact them personally. Therefore you may get negative or questioning reactions. These reactions may even be framed in what seem like positive words.

When Kim tried to make changes a year ago she was told to be careful because people would be watching her closely to see if she succeeded or not. She was told that she is what she is—very sweet. Kim was also told; "You're a darling and don't try to become a 'toughie'. People may not like you in your new role. Another comment was, "Oh dear, you've tried this before haven't you? It's so hard to change."

This time around Kim did not share her goals with anyone. She knew that when the changes were made people would see her in a different light and would have to judge her on her results.

4. Eliminate the word "change."

Replace it with any of these easily doable words:
Adjust –– Alter — Amend — Adapt

This is especially important if you are a manager or leader. When you use the word change fear arises. When you're about to change actions, procedures, systems, or any initiatives don't use the word "change." So, let's say you are changing the sales goal for the year. Present it this way: "We are moving our target goal to $__ so that we can adjust sales to encompass our new product line and ease our customers into better solutions."

Kim decided not to use the word change and instead began to think of the word "alteration." She thought to herself: When I make alterations to my jackets or pants I don't change the whole structure of the garment I simply change a part of the garment so that it will fit me better. That's how Kim viewed her approach to improvement—an alteration.

5. **List three small incremental action steps to take each day.**

To avoid fearing change—the BIG change—think of change as incremental—small and slow. Think of change as "small change"—as coins in your pocket or wallet. These coins are small—nowhere as big as the dollar bills you carry.

Bank of America has a program called *Keep the Change*®. Once you sign up for the program every time you make a purchase using your BOA card they will round up your total amount to the nearest dollar and the difference—the small change [as in coins] goes into your account. Well, you know what happens over time; all the small change turns into big bills.

Kim made a list of small incremental adjustments to her work and her behaviors. She started by not allowing anyone to interrupt her when she was speaking. She would raise her hand slightly and simply say; "Please allow me to finish my points." She then followed up in writing the ideas she presented and her action plan so there was no mistaking whose ideas were whose. The last incremental step for Kim was to simply look people in the eye when they were speaking to her—slowly eliminating the perception of Kim being shy.

These small incremental steps eventually lead to big results.

6. Maintain flexibility

Sometimes the best-laid plans don't work as we expect. Don't be hard on yourself. Rather, expect that things won't always work according to plan. This way if they do work you'll be pleased and if they don't you won't be disappointed. Keep altering, adapting, and adjusting. Keep moving toward your goal.

One of Kim's ideas was to make suggestions on changing the format of the weekly staff meetings to make them more productive. After making the suggestions Kim was asked what was wrong with her? Kim was taken aback by the response but realized that maybe she hadn't gone about making the suggestions in the right way. She decided to put this effort aside for the time being and pursue it at a later time.

7. **Reward yourself along the way.**

In my workshops I ask people to pair with another person. Once people are coupled I ask them to stand and face each other and quickly do a visual evaluation of each other. I then ask them to stand back-to-back and to make some changes in their personal appearance. Once they do this I now ask them to face each other again and note any changes they each made to their appearance. The most common changes include taking off glasses, removing jewelry or a jacket, rolling up shirt sleeves, pulling hair down from a clip, unbuttoning a shirt collar and so on. After a few more steps in the exercise I ask the people who made changes by subtracting, removing, or eliminating something to stand up. Most stand. Then I ask who made changes by adding something. Only a few stand. I then ask why we inevitably take something away when we are asked to make changes. The point that always resonates with my audience is that change can mean addition as well as subtraction. Think of adding to what you already do and thus expand your strengths rather than trying to replace any of them.

OWN IT:

- What would you most like to change in your life? How willing are you to make these changes?
- When will you make them?
- What's your biggest piece of "unfinished business" ... personally or professionally?

- What brings you the greatest happiness? How are you going to make sure, you have more of that happiness in your life?
- And, perhaps, the most challenging question: What is the risk of doing nothing?

CHAPTER TWELVE

Trust is a Must

Commitments. Collaboration. Confidence. What do these three C words have in common? They're all about TRUST—the single most important factor of your reputation—your brand—who you are and how others see you. Trust is the solid rock on which all relationships and commitments are built. Friends, families, marriages, and work relationships all depend on honesty and integrity. Trust means confidence in and reliance on strong qualities, especially fairness, truth, honor, and ability. You can be the brightest, the best in what you do, the most charismatic—but if other's don't trust you, you have nothing.

Absence of trust exhibits itself in guarded communication, cautious actions, protective measures, and avoidance of risk. Collaboration becomes defensive and caution prevents exploration of ideas and therefore growth. The consequences quickly lead to disengagement and erosion of passion for both your job and your company. Trust is a two way street. Who do you trust or not trust and who trusts you or doesn't? The more people you trust and rely on the more you will love what you do.

The results of not being trusted can be devastating. They may include loss of integrity, derailed career opportunities, diminished credibility, tarnished reputation, and damaged relationships. Once trust is lost it is very difficult to regain. That's why you must focus on building trust from the very first day on your job regardless of your position or title. And if you're already in a job, but never really thought about the impact trust may have on your job, then it's time to reconsider.

Every one of us is where we are today because someone we trusted helped us, taught us, or pointed the way. Management is now embracing this belief. Companies and organizations are placing strong emphasis on people development through relationships. Research points out that people stay in jobs when they form good relationships with their co-workers. Succession planning programs are becoming more important and vital to an organization's ongoing success. Coaching strategies are being taught. Mentoring is encouraged and supported by management. A new awareness has developed of how our trusted relationships can work to grow our businesses and ourselves. Regardless of the business you're in, people—namely customers and employees—are its lifeblood. They can help you or hurt you. I've found that many of us forget the impact others have had on our success. Most of us remember to say "thank you" for the latest referral, recommendation, or praise. But how often do we trace the origin of someone who placed enough faith in our potential to help us? How did we meet him or her? Who was responsible for initiating the relationship? What would have happened if we had not met that person? I compare this process to creating a family tree.

The Trust Tree

This discovery led me to develop my "Trust Tree™" exercise, which I use when working with senior management on mentoring and leadership skills. I ask all participants to trace the roots of relationships that impacted their careers or business successes. Here's how this process works:

YOUR TRUST TREE

1. Think of a recent success.
2. Identify the individual that helped you (directly or indirectly) to achieve this success.
3. Recall how you met this person.
4. Think of who initiated or facilitated this encounter. It could be an individual or a group.
5. Picture your actions as a result of this encounter.
6. Continue this process as far back as you can remember.
7. Start this process over again by recalling other successful achievements.

While conducting a recent management workshop, I witnessed the impact of this process on the participants. I decided it was time for me to draw another "Trust Tree" of my own. The experience was powerful. I recalled people I hadn't spoken with in years. I remembered lessons painfully learned and the "teachers" who demonstrated their trust by standing by me. I relived the support of an acquaintance who became a close friend, and of a client whose one referral (five years earlier) continues to provide a steady source of income. I began to contact my trusted sources. A few I could not locate. One had died. The rest were more than happy to hear from me. All were thrilled about my successes, and pleased to recall the roles they'd played in my life. A surprising result from this effort— new doors opened, new relationships developed, and a new lesson was learned. A former mentor, now 70-some years young, told me, "You should go back to your tree more often. Every year it bears new fruit!"

As you coach and mentor others while growing your work life, career, or your business, use this method to subtly emphasize the importance of trusted relationships to your successes. Managers who use this process with their employees also discover a renewed team spirit and more emphasis on the importance of each individual they have met.

One Success Story

Here is how one business owner—a specialty retailer with 46 stores— used, and continues to use, this process to attract and retain new employees. He asks all store managers to recall how they found their best employees. In many cases, good hires were the result of referrals from customers or employees. He then asks managers to consider how they met the person who initiated the referral. The managers are at this point creating their own Trust Tree. The owner then creates an initiative for the store managers to see who can develop the tallest and thickest of trees.

Managers use their Trust Tree to reach out and contact people with whom they hadn't spoken to in a long time. Six months into the process, the owner reported that the process is a great success. He cites:

- A 40% drop in turnover
- Improved quality of hires

- Increased productivity
- Revived contact with previous customers who created new business
- A waiting list of job applicants

As in most businesses, we are constantly developing new approaches to reach new customers and new employees. Contacting people who already know us, who have shown their trust in us and supported us in the past is an effective and rewarding approach. I suggest you take time to draw your own "Trust Tree." Then take the time to say "thank you." Remind those who have trusted and helped you that you will not forget your valued sources of success.

How Do You Build Trust?

Keep Promises. Without thinking, you repeatedly make promises daily. But do you keep them? Trust erosion occurs as a result of unkept promises. Repeated often they become your brand—your signature. What follows is "Don't believe what he tells you" or "If he says tomorrow you're lucky to get it next week." From "I'll get you those numbers" to "I'll call the customer and straighten this out ..." if you don't keep track of the fly-by comments you won't do what you said you would and you become labeled.

Marcia is in the elevator. On the next floor Jack gets in the elevator and says to Marcia; "Hey, by the way, you know that marketing meeting we're having next Friday? I'd like to get a copy of that last presentation you did for ADA. Can you just copy me on it? I can't seem to find my copy. Marcia replies, "Sure, not a problem."

Fast forward to the meeting on Friday when Marcia sees Jack and remembers that she forgot to send him what he asked for. She walks over to Jack and apologizes. Jack shrugs with a "whatever" comment. Marcia remembers that she also made a few other promises to other people in conjunction with this marketing meeting. Justifying her failure to follow through she thinks to herself, "I just can't keep track of all these things that people constantly want from me." She too is busy. "Why can't people just work a little harder and get their own information?"

How far will this attitude take Marcia? How long before others stop asking her for information because they perceive her as unreliable? How long before people will start saying to others that you can't trust Marcia to get anything done?

You may think to yourself—hey not a bad thing. People will finally stop bugging Marcia for stuff. Believe me—I can relate. There is a bit of humor in this. But is that an effective way to get along—build relationships—be perceived as an "A" player—get promoted—be respected? I don't think so!

So Marcia has three options—she could have used either one with Jack. Marcia can also use these options with anyone to ensure that when she makes a promise she keeps it and becomes known as a trustworthy person.

Option 1. If Marcia truly feels that she's being bothered with requests from people who are simply too lazy to get what they need themselves—a peer in another department or a co-worker—[not your boss!] she should put the burden on the person making the request. For instance she should have asked Jack to send her an email requesting specifically what he was looking for in the presentation that Marcia did for ADA. I have found that many times people will make requests of others because it's easy to do when you see someone—and then they later forget all about it. Or when the burden is put on them to remember their requests they just simply don't follow up.

Option 2. Whenever Marcia leaves her workspace she should always carry a tool to jot down reminders, requests from others, or simply random thoughts that might occur to her when she least expects them. A small notebook, digital recorder, or any mobile device will work. Most promises are broken through simple forgetfulness rather than lack of time or other constraints. If a request is made and Marcia decides to follow through then she needs to immediately note the request and the dates or times she has agreed to. It is also okay for Marcia to respond by explaining that she's not sure she can meet that request—or she needs to think about it before committing. But she will get back to that person by a mutually agreed to time and then she jots that down.

Option 3. Quite often people tend to minimize a request or will ask a question that truly requires more thought and discussion then can be given during a "fly by." The reasons for "catching" you in this manner may vary but I have found they include:

- Asking for your decision quickly because if you were given more time you may oppose it.

- Asking if you'll have time later for a quick meeting regarding an important issue. You may respond, "sure" and "let me know when" without knowing what the issue is or how long it will take—or even if you will have the time.
- Catching you off guard with a statement that is a "done deal." This usually starts off with a "by the way …" **Ex:** "Oh, by the way Marcia, when you were out yesterday we decided to move ahead and confirm the proposal on … We couldn't wait."

These examples compromise trust. You shouldn't allow them to happen to you. You also should never practice using these tactics yourself.

If you find yourself in any of these situations, stop them immediately. A simple action of raising your hand and saying; "I feel the issue you're telling me about needs a little more discussion then I have time for right now." Then schedule a time for more discussion.

People are often in a rush and request things or agree to requests just to keep things moving. This especially happens in what I call "fly bys"—quick conversations or quick stops in the hallways or elevators—before and after meetings—walking into the office in the morning or leaving at night. When this happens there is a great risk not to follow through and when that happens, trust erodes. So be cautious of "fly-by" requests. This is a time to remember your Trust Tree®.

I was coaching Mark, a Sales Director for a pharmaceutical company, on how to be more proficient in his use of time when he told me that he gets inundated with multiple requests before he even gets to his office in the morning. Mark then began to use the Options I listed above to manage all these requests and found that these "fly-by" requests diminished substantially and that he reduced his anxiety about trying to remember what he promised people.

Mark also learned that it actually saves a lot of time to stop for an extra minute and pinpoint a person's "fly-by" request and agree to an outcome rather than do what most people do and simply yell out "sure - no problem."

How Do You Repair Trust?

According to behavioral research trust is implied in many relationships. For instance, when a person is hired the team members and the boss *trust* the new employee to do a good job, to be fair and honest, and to keep promises. They will trust what the person tells them and trust the reliability of their information. People with certain behavioral styles trust others intrinsically while other styles delay the extent of trust until they have proven to themselves that a person is trustworthy. Whether a person's trust factor is totally trusted or somewhat trusted will quickly plummet when and if the trust is compromised.

OWN IT:

- If you know you have lost someone's trust the only thing to do is to begin repairing that loss. This begins with the words "I'm sorry".
- Create your "Trust Tree" and go back to thank the people who helped you grow and develop—people who believed in you and trusted you.

Although it is possible to rebuild trust, never forget what Warren Buffett said: "It takes twenty years to build a reputation and five minutes to ruin it."

CHAPTER THIRTEEN

Momentum Moments

When was the last time you stood in front of a mirror, looked at yourself and said out loud, "boy, that was a job well done"? Or just simply "you did it!"

When I pose this question to people—be they managers, executives or line workers— some look at me like I'm crazy—some laugh—others say, "You're not serious are you?" Then of course I have to explain. We look to others to validate us, to give us positive feedback, to bolster us up. Very few people rely on themselves for this type of reinforcement. And yet it's probably the most important thing you can do for yourself. Why don't we focus more on ourselves? Why don't we regularly recognize our inner strengths and instead, seem to need this acknowledgement from others? We don't because this reliance on others to make us feel good began at an early age. This validation may have come from parents, teachers, friends, family members, or coaches. We have a desire to be praised and recognized.

Unfortunately, as we get older these sources of praise diminish. Who do you rely on today for your pats on the back? Perhaps it's a spouse— some friends—some family. The reality is that as an adult not many people sing your praises. Therefore the "mirror moment" arrives; the self-validation time when you tell yourself that you are good and that you do good.

I often ask my audiences what they think of when they're driving home. Most will say they think of what they didn't get to complete during the day. Many recall some of the workplace conflicts, disagreements, or disappointments with others. But mostly we think negative thoughts. We are programmed to attract and dwell on the negative. Our brains treat negative thoughts like Velcro®—it sticks. The positive thoughts get treated like Teflon®—they just roll off. As a result we have to re-program ourselves to focus on the positives. This doesn't just happen automatically. This is important because your beliefs determine your thoughts, which in turn impact your behavior. So learn to catch yourself at your best moments. Learn to be more like yourself at your very best moments. Learn to congratulate yourself and use your "mirror moments' often.

Dulce, a young woman who worked very hard to get herself moved up within an organization finally became the Director of HR. She started in the company as an Administrative Assistant. She then set a goal to receive her certifications in behavioral and motivator assessments. This was no small feat because she had to not only study but also be coached for many hours in addition to working sixty plus hours a week. She was finally ready to take her exams but at the same time was terrified that she wouldn't pass.

Well she did—she passed with flying colors. I had the opportunity and pleasure to explain her achievement at a large company meeting and she received a standing ovation. The CEO praised her further explaining how she believed in herself and pushed herself to win. It truly was a shining moment for her and she just beamed in the acknowledgement of her accomplishment. I asked her how she felt. She told me that she felt so proud of herself. She kept congratulating herself over and over. No matter who praised her—even the CEO—it could never match how she felt inside herself.

Your greatest motivator and your best acknowledgements reside within you so look in that mirror and praise yourself out loud.

You may feel you don't receive enough information or you don't get enough advice or direction. Perhaps you don't get an opportunity to learn and develop new skills or you don't get acknowledgement for your contributions. You're not alone. I hear these complaints at all levels of an organization—from senior managers to contributors. These omissions are always the result and fault of someone else. But is it?

Let's step away from the average workplace and look inside the walls of hospitals or rehabilitation centers. Here we encounter patients who either because of an accident or disease are trying to regain movements or strengths that previously were taken for granted or never even thought about—something as relatively simple as turning your head or motioning with a finger. I know something about this due to personal experiences and I clearly remember doctors, nurses, and physical therapists telling me that given the same care—the same advice—the same treatments, some patients take charge of getting better while others blame the system—their misfortune—their caretakers. The key words are "take charge." So the question is are you taking charge or are you blaming outcomes on something or someone else? What are your choices?

Believe in Yourself

It was a typical ending to a fabulous skiing day in the tiny town of Woodstock, Vermont on Valentine's Day, February 14. A bunch of my family and friends were relaxing with hot toddies, mulled wine, beer and of course my favorite – a glass of Chardonnay. This was our annual get-away in February and this year we had a big reason to celebrate because my brother John passed his New York and New Jersey bar exams and he did so on his first try. If you know a law student or a lawyer they'll tell you that this is a major accomplishment. We were extra proud because just a few years before then we didn't think he would ever make college. Now we had a lawyer!

We were all in high spirits when we noticed the ski patrol bringing someone down on a sled. We expressed surprise because they were coming down the "Bunny Run"—a beginner's slope. A ski instructor walked into the Lodge and said; "I think something happened to one of yours." We all rushed out and sure enough it was John on the sled – unconscious. He was rushed to the local hospital then transferred to the Dartmouth Medical Center where we later learned that John's ski had gone out from under him and he had landed on a tree stump severing his spinal cord. For days the doctor's worked on him just to keep him alive. The doctors graphically explained to me that John's nerves were similar to a bunch of thin gold chains thrown into a pile and which you must then try to unravel. Weeks later when John was stabilized he was transported to the Craig Institute in Denver, Colorado for rehabilitation.

I visited John frequently while he was at the Craig Institute, met with his doctors, and learned about the tough road John had ahead of him as a paraplegic. John had no feeling below his waist and would never walk again. His recovery would also be more mental than physical. He had choices—feeling sorry for himself or accepting his fate and learning how to live a different life. John struggled and didn't speak with me during several visits. When we finally talked I asked him if he felt ready to go out for a ride and see Pike's Peak. If I had known what this would involve I would never have suggested it. I had no clue! It was John's first lesson and experience in getting in and out of a car without the use of his legs. It took him 45 minutes to get in the car, but off we went. We even had lunch at the restaurant at Pike's Peak when I noticed John was getting very tired—and rapidly. We returned to Craig's Institute and John quickly fell asleep.

Days later we started talking about his future plans to return to New Jersey. John lived in a tiny apartment that was not very accessible so plans needed to be made. Before John's accident he clerked for a judge. The judge told John that he had his job back if he wanted it and John accepted. This judge became an angel to John.

A few years later John opened up his own practice and quickly became the local "Perry Mason" practicing law in his wheelchair. His practice flourished and he brought on partners. Meanwhile he also decided to breed, raise, and train beagles. On weekends he would bring four to six dogs to dog shows up and down the East Coast—and he did it all by himself—loading and unloading the dogs and their cages in arenas without help. He won tons of ribbons and then one day, the biggest win of all—"Best of Breed" at the Westminster Dog Show in Madison Square Garden in New York City. John had a dog handler for a while but soon built up the skill and fortitude to show the dogs himself—in his wheelchair. No small feat.

Then while practicing law and being a breeder and trainer, John also decided to start a web-based business—"Uncle Dave's Trains"—where he began to buy and sell brass model trains. John built this into a major Internet business. www.Uncledavesbrass.com.

John then married a high school friend and they decided to adopt a child. Knowing the hardships of being handicapped John and his wife, Maryann decided to adopt a child who had disabilities. Both John and Maryann's lives were steeped in Polish backgrounds and traditions—John speaks Polish fluently—and so they decided to travel to an orphanage in Poland. Here they adopted a seven year old named Peter who had lived in an orphanage since he was barely a year old—given up by a very young mother who could no longer care for him. John and Maryann took on a major challenge with this adoption because Peter was handicapped in several areas. As the years passed they have all grown incredibly, both as a family and as individuals. My brother continues to be an incredible role model for me; especially when I force myself to compare my day-to-day challenges to his. Why? Because at a pivotal point in his life he had a choice and he chose to "take charge."

OWN IT

Ask yourself:

- Do you have the ambition to go out and learn more about what it takes to be better—do your job better—to produce more than what is simply required of you?
- Have you grown complacent waiting for others to provide to you and for you?

- When is the last time you asked to be invited to a meeting that you normally don't attend?
- Are you aware of your strengths and are you using them every day or are you more focused on your weaknesses—trying to improve in areas only because you feel inadequate.
- What skills does your job require? Are they matched to your current skills?
- Have you congratulated yourself recently on at least one fabulous achievement? Do you do this regularly—at least once a week?
- What more could you do to truly take charge?

CHAPTER FOURTEEN

Reliable Reporting

We often get so involved with our own lives that we miss what's going on around us. Who's doing what? Who's saying what? It is impossible to achieve passion and love for what you do if you are focused solely on yourself. Little in life can be accomplished alone. Others impact your chances for success. They can also be detrimental to you achieving your goals. Knowing who you can help is as important as asking others for help. This is the secret of people who excel in networking, branding, and marketing themselves.

Begin to act more like a reporter to learn about what's really going on in your workplace. Learn to use **small talk** to identify underlying motives of others, including your boss.

"Small talk"-- *One of the most frequently asked questions and requests that I receive while coaching others is how do you make small talk. I'll often ask the person to define what they think small talk is. The answer is usually the ability to speak with people who you don't know in order to meet people, make friends, and not feel isolated. This is usually a problem for people when they are at a meeting, a conference, trade show, a party, or any gathering filled with strangers. I ask, if you ever tried to do this, how did you begin and what were the results? The answers range from making a statement about the weather, recent national events, or [usually with men] comments about recent sports related news. This is when I offer a suggestion: small talk is not about talking. And that's how most people perceive small talk—the ability to talk. The skill of small talk is all about asking questions. Small talk is the ability to get the person with whom you are trying to engage to comment about themselves or their ideas, or to ask you a question that opens the flow of communication. I recommend that a person think about the event they are attending and plan a few questions in advance.*

EX: Attending a conference: What was the best meeting that you attended so far? What made it so good? Who are you looking forward to hearing next? Do you have a plan on how you organize and handle the information that you gather?

Be ready to reciprocate the answers to these questions if you are asked.

This formula works well for any gathering.

EX: At a party: How did you meet the host/hostess? Have you met any of the people attending? Do you live in this area? Try not to succumb to the standard "what do you do" question. When you get to know the person a little better this may be appropriate.

There is also a time when it's time to move on. Don't manipulate the person's time because you begin to feel comfortable and safe with them. Move on and find a person who is standing alone—there are always plenty of those who feel the same way you do—afraid of small talk. You will be honing your small talk skills and will begin to relax and enjoy yourself. You will also feel a sense of accomplishment and pride and look forward to the next event you attend.

By being a reporter you learn to transition your thinking from your perceptions into reality. I have a saying that I often use when people fervently claim that perception is reality. I say: "Perception is reality – only for the ignorant." This is harsh but it gets people's attention. I explain that when people don't have the facts and the correct data they then assume that what they know is the truth. When you have all the facts and the data then you have reality and there is no room for perceptions. I have repeated this concept several times in this book. That's because I firmly believe in my motto "repeat to remember".

You are now ready to become the reporter and learn more about the reality of your workplace.

How you do this is by copying the formula that has worked as a model for reporters for decades. Even when you search the Internet this is the model that makes up a lot of the information you receive.

Who

Who are the people others go to for help—and this is not always the boss. I call these folks the "underground leaders"—not necessarily people with a title but definitely full of knowledge. Who do you rely on?

What

What are people concerned about? What are they talking about? What is the current hot topic—and this is not necessarily about the company or current projects. What are their expectations of you?

Where

Where's the focus? Where are others going with projects—and this is not always what's been laid out in the "strategic plans." Where are customers coming from?

When

When do others expect to get things done—and this is not always what they tell the boss or team members.

Why

Why are workers talking about certain things that may not be obvious to others? Why are rumors spreading? Why do certain departments and people not communicate with one another?

Toxic Talk—Gossip and Rumors

Imagine if reporters—true reporters or journalists not sensationalists—relied on rumors or gossip to create the stories we hear on our trusted news sources. What would happen to their credibility? Could you rely on them for the truth? The same is true for you. What happens in the workplace when people gossip or spread rumors? What's the result of toxic talk and how does it impact the team and morale? How does it inevitably impact you?

As an executive coach and business advisor I have witnessed how toxic talk can lead to stress and even depression. Talented and engaged people can become unproductive and lose their passion and love for what they do simply because of other's perceptions due to toxic talk.

Sarah is a senior accountant in the business department for a large hospital chain. Jane, her immediate boss is the assistant comptroller and Nathan is the comptroller. Although Sarah interacts with Nathan on many issues, it is Jane that she must inevitably report to. Sarah loves the challenging work, is extremely competent and is often complimented by Nathan for being proactive about recommending efficiency tactics. But after less than a year on the job Sarah has begun to dread going to work. And it's all because of Jane's negative attitude and foul language.

Nearly every day Jane brings up the fact that she can't wait until she can retire because the job is just killing her. She complains constantly to her subordinates about the job and many of the people who work there. And she uses language unacceptable to any workplace. At first Sarah just tried to shrug it off but the intensity of Jane's toxic language, negativity and constant interruptions began to stress and depress her. Sarah finally mustered up enough courage to talk to Nathan about the situation. He acknowledged the problem but did little to resolve it. Finally Sarah told Nathan she was going to human resources about Jane's language because she just couldn't tolerate it any more. Jane's inappropriate language was even impacting Sarah's assistant and there had already been quite a bit of turnover in support staff. Nathan supported her decision to go to H.R.

> *After going to human resources, Jane was talked to and she did stop using some of her inappropriate language. But her constant complaining and negativity continued. Nathan says he'd like to make some changes but because of Jane's length of employment he feels he can't. Sarah believes that Nathan is a weak manager and therefore little will change. So, as much as she loves the overall business and the work that she does, Sarah has decided to quietly look for a new position.*

The unfortunate realities of this situation are all negatively impacting the accounting department. Efficiency is declining, morale is suffering, productivity is falling, turnover is highly probable and loss of a capable, highly valued talent is very much at risk. Yes there are human resource issues to contend with in dealing with the toxic individual. Yet without addressing the problem effectively, much is at risk.

Rumors and gossip also set the stage for negative impact.

> *Lori is extremely analytical, diligent and highly focused on her job in production control. Her dedication to resolving problems and producing results, have earned Lori praise and recognition from her boss. But because of Lori's extremely serious personality, she has little desire to be outgoing and friendly. Her co-workers find her unfriendly, detached and extremely contained. Although they know little about Lori's personal life, their perception is that she has no real life outside of work and most likely has this job because her lack of personality did not afford her many options.*

> *Based on pure perceptions, co-workers began to gossip about Lori. One day Lori overheard two co-workers discussing Lori in unfavorable terms, even calling her a derogatory name. Hurt more than angered by what she overheard, Lori reported the incident to her boss. To Lori, his response was less than supportive. While he disapproved of the name-calling he pointed out to Lori that she was unfriendly, remained isolated and made no attempts to be part of the team.*
>
> *"Are you pleased with the work I do?" Lori asked. With little hesitation the boss confirmed that he was very pleased with her work. With that Lori explained that she believed she should be judged on her performance, not her personality. The boss responded that she was part of a team and therefore how she interacted was equally important.*
>
> *Within the year Lori quit her job.*

Here's a situation where no one, even Lori's boss, was able to respect the difference of behavior styles. Admittedly Lori was ideally suited to her job and performed it competently and proficiently. But because her behavior style was different than her co-workers, she was judged harshly. When these unfair judgments are made good people are hurt and, as in the case of Lori, the company looses a good person ideally suited to the job.

Gossip, rumors and toxic people are detriments to any work environment. When these exist it is difficult to love your job. Productive and happy employees act like reporters; they get the facts, deal with the truth, and behave respectfully which allows everyone to love their job.

OWN IT:

- By gathering and understanding the information you receive from others, you become more knowledgeable and valuable to others.
- By asking questions, as you learned to do through "small talk," you will replace your perceptions with reality.
- Be proactive as a reporter. Ask to be invited to meetings that you don't normally attend.
- Form a networking or mastermind group. Meet regularly and discuss the issues that each member of the group needs help with. Ask what specifically you can do to help—don't just offer to help.
- People spend a lot of time listening to toxic talk, and rumors—also creating them. Therefore, gather a group of people you trust and choose a rumor that has recently surfaced. Then get the facts—and start "rumors" that will dispel, correct, or overpower the ones that are out there and are incorrect. You will be amazed at the power of reliable rumors.
- Socrates said that the primary virtue is courage, for without that you can't employ any other virtue. Have the courage to do what's right.

CHAPTER FIFTEEN

Juggling Generations

There are currently four major generations in today's workforce—soon there will be five. They are identified as the Traditionalists, Baby Boomers, Generation X, and the Millennials. Each generation brings to the workplace different work modes, communication styles, motivators, managerial methods, and expectations. Each generation has unique needs as well. Most of these are all shaped by events and trends that occurred during their upbringing. Therefore conflicts can occur. Working with these differences is a challenge for everyone—regardless of your position. There are also differences within each generation—not all people fall exactly into the descriptors. Recognize that everybody does not act like their peers within a generation. However, members of each generation bring to the workforce similar styles and experiences. The descriptors of each generation form a framework to use as a guideline in helping you understand each generation. Start by identifying the generation that you belong to.

Let's look at the values of the first two generations and what they bring to the workplace. These are the people who for the most part have already left the workplace or will soon be leaving.

Traditionalists

The Traditionalists, also known as Veterans, Matures, the Silent Generation and the Greatest Generation, are those workers born between 1922 and 1945 and number roughly 75 million people. Their core values are a strong work ethic, dedication, privacy, brand loyalty, tradition, honor, respect and sacrifice.

Traditionalists tend to be logical, conservative, conformist, and historical. They hold themselves and others accountable. The events and trends that shaped this generation were patriotism, families, the Great Depression, World War II and the Korean War, as well as the Golden Age of Radio.

Traditionalists believe in a lifetime career with a single employer. They expect to have lifetime employment, to do a good job, to have opportunities for growth within the organization and for the employer to take care of them.

Traditionalists adhere to the company's rules, regulations, policies and procedures. They have pride in themselves for being hard workers and have respect for authority. They feel work is an obligation. They also respect seniority and feel their years of experience deserve respect. The leadership style used is direct and commanding and the organizational structure is formal.

Traditionalists prefer communicating one-on-one, in person or by telephone, or in writing through messages. They do not expect, require or need ongoing praise in their jobs. This generation tends to be technically challenged.

Baby Boomers

Baby Boomers, also known simply as Boomers, are those workers born between 1946 and 1964 and number roughly 76 million people. Their core values are optimism, teamwork, personal gratification, contribution, involvement, anti-rules and regulation, competition and success, hard work, and personal growth.

Boomers tend to be driven, willing to go the extra mile for success, have a love/hate relationship with authority, are willing to fight for a cause, like to be 'up to date' and 'in the know' and accept people—as long as those people meet their standards. The events and trends that shaped this generation were prosperity, television, suburbia, assassinations, the Vietnam War and Civil Rights. These are the children of the Traditionalists and early on in their development swore that they would not resemble their parents. To their surprise they often look in the mirror and see their mother or father staring back at them—sharing their parent's values as they get older.

This is the generation that should be retiring but due to the uncertainty of the economy are trying to hold on to their jobs. As a result they are impeding the company's promotion process of the following generations causing angst and frustration within the new generations. And they are the parents of the new generations—Gen X and the Millennials.

The New Generations

The up and coming members of the new generations hold a very different outlook on life—on their expectations—on relationships—and their needs. These are governed by the technological advances made during their formative years and by the independence forced on them by their working parents. They consider themselves grown up by the ages of 24 to 30—very different from their parents and grandparents who were forced to grow up and accept responsibilities by the ages of 16 to 18. The Millennials specifically have no problem in moving back with their parents after finishing school and staying there until they feel they're ready to move on.

Gen X

This generation is well known as the 'latchkey kids'. Born between 1965 and 1980 they grew up with both parents working and no daycare as we know it today. Society's focus on up and coming technology excited them and involved them. Desktop adding machines were replaced by calculators, mimeograph machines were replaced by high-speed copiers and faxes were sent in seconds rather than many minutes. Room size computers were laughed at by Gen Xers when they got their desktops.

They valued independence and many times exhibited superiority over their parents who they treated more as friends than parents. Many times they were bounced back and forth between parents because of ever increasing divorces. They number approximately 49 million and when compared to Baby Boomers and the Millennials represent a very small chunk of the population.

Gen Xers plan to have six to eleven jobs in their lifetime. They value their independence—many times want to work alone rather than in a team. They want to know that their contributions are important to their bosses and the company. They are not impressed with titles or authority. They embrace diversity and accept differences in others. Personal health and family responsibilities top their list of needs.

Millennials

Also known as 'Gen Y', this generation is the most talked about, most researched, and most misunderstood. Pick up a newspaper, magazine, or watch a TV talk show and you'll read or hear something about Millennials.

- By 2015 there were 46 million Millennials in the workforce with another 34 million on their way.
- They tend to mature and accept responsibilities at a later age—most likely the age of 30.
- They will hold approximately fifteen to thirty jobs in their lifetime.
- Their attitudes and behaviors are shaped by the Gulf War, Columbine, the dot com bust, 9/11, the Wall Street meltdown, and Bin Laden.
- They're quite diverse with fifteen percent of them being born in a foreign country.

- They are shaped by technology and as a result are multi taskers, quick learners, and want lots of information.
- Mostly influenced by their parents and peers they are constantly in touch via electronics and social media.
- They do not automatically respect traditional authority—they question everything.

As I have learned over the past few years most of the information about Millennials is incorrect—at best—and misleading. In my opinion, the best research I've seen on Gen Y comes from two people, Bette Price and Mark Holmes. Both have done their research and truly understand the men and woman of this generation, which is overtaking the Baby Boomers by millions. The Millennials are and will be impacting not only the workforce but also our trends in food, entertainment, technology, and culture. Born between 1980 and 2000—specific years identified by the U. S. Census Bureau—this generation is accused of being impatient, having a poor work ethic, needing constant praise, being disrespectful, lacking motivation, and having a sense of entitlement. My question—so what's new? Speaking from a Baby Boomer's perspective this is exactly how I was perceived by my parents, teachers, and bosses. So let's look at facts rather than perceptions and opinions about this generation.

The research and resulting White Paper done by Price and Holmes is available in great detail on www.GenBlending.com. I will highlight some of their findings that answer the questions I'm most often asked. How do I manage, communicate with, and understand this group of people who are so different from me? The short answer is that they are not so different from you—they simply are more vocal and more impatient. If you look at these descriptors from a positive perspective they're actually what companies need today in the world of customers and consumers who want what they want today! Ask yourself – are you impatient? Do you want to wait in lines? Do you want instant gratification and immediate results? The Millennials represent these needs and it behooves the companies they work for to capture and encourage their perspectives and their need to get things done quickly. Therefore impatience is not a negative but a positive when applied to the results that you desire.

If you are a Baby Boomer who is managing a Millennial it's to your advantage to gain a better understanding of this person's communication pattern and work style. Failing to respond to a Millennial's need for trust and transparency will lead to greater turnover and poor morale. If you are a Millennial it will greatly help you to understand that there are generational differences and you need to understand these in order to accomplish what you set out to do and make the impact that you desire.

Here are some facts from the Price and Holmes research:

Passion plays a huge role. Results from a measurable assessment shows that practicality, results, and collaboration tremendously impact their desire to do what they love. A huge 93 percent would leave a job for opportunities to do work for which they have a passion—despite a possible lessening of pay. Significance is also significant in their willingness to stay. They want to know that they contribute to the overall, which is why 82 percent would leave if their boss failed to value their opinions or ideas. They understand that they have much to learn, yet to be dismissed for merely not being old enough or on the job long enough makes little sense to them at all. To them, performance trumps experience. Given the opportunity to be involved, to learn, to contribute, they expect to be judged on their ability to contribute and perform.

- 86% want challenging, rewarding work
- 54% want to know they contribute to an overall mission

This is a generation that excels in quick adaptability, armed with the ability to research thoroughly for new, innovative possibilities. They are nimble and highly equipped technologically to connect in short periods of time. Who better than this generation to be innovative?

This generation is motivated to make a difference and to achieve results. Without the opportunities to play a significant role, they become quickly disenchanted. While often accused of having little respect for their elders, the reality is that this generation, more than any other before them, have tremendous respect for their parents and grandparents—thus co-workers of those generations. However there is a real disconnect when seasoned workers fail to equally respect the ideas and concepts that these younger individuals bring forth in a sincere effort to seek improvements or innovation.

As Walt Disney believed, when you blend the old with the new, you get new again. Experienced individuals who are open to encouraging and truly hearing new thinking will find great value in blending the old and the new. But that takes an open mind and a willingness to believe that experience alone is no predictor or guarantee of success. Because this generation is so motivated by performance, versus experience, they are ideally poised for a "pay for performance" structure.

There is a definite shift in how time is valued with this generation. Having grown up to see their generation of parents fall prey to downsizing, right-sizing, and cutbacks or suffer the losses of a shifting economy, this generation isn't about to give up their quest to devote important time to family and friends only to be easily dismissed as their parents were. But, that doesn't mean they are not committed to meeting goals and accomplishing tasks.

Time becomes irrelevant from the standpoint that this generation's philosophy is: Tell me what needs to be accomplished and within what time frame and I will do that. Meeting the deadline with results is what counts, not merely putting in standardized hours. That means that if a young father leaves early to be present at his son's basketball game, he will do what it takes to make up that time to ensure that the task is accomplished within the given time frame. To him, it's all about results.

- 79% want to work with independence
- 80% want flexibility in their work schedule
- 79% would leave the job if they are micromanaged

"We're willing to pay our dues, but not the dues older generations paid—like broken families, parents who were workaholics, suffered bad health, etc. Either we experienced seeing this or our friends did. We'll pay our dues differently."

This generation wants to know that they have contributed to overall results; that whatever the role they play, their contribution has been integral to achieving a desired outcome. This doesn't mean that every role has to be defined as highly significant. It does, however, mean that it is critical to involve, challenge and acknowledge their contributions as well as inform them as to the overall significance that even their small, menial task may play in "making a difference."

How does their role contribute to the greater whole? This may not have been important to other generations who may have been task-focused on a particular job. It means everything to this generation who are driven to make a difference and to know how their efforts contribute to the overall. Here is a case in point:

> *Raymond was asked by the sales manager to collate a number of printed pages of a presentation into spiral bound books. No more information was given to Raymond—simply a directive to complete the bound books and have them ready by five that evening. Raymond complied and met his deadline. The next afternoon the sales manager haphazardly mentioned to Raymond that he appreciated the job he had done and mentioned that the booklets had been used for a critical presentation to a major client earlier that day which resulted in securing a huge new piece of business. While Raymond was pleased to find out that his efforts had helped in landing the new business, he pointed out: "I was happy to do what they asked, but I would have felt so much better about completing the task had I known up front how important my small role was to the overall goal."*

Despite the perception that this generation's penchant for seeming to isolate themselves through their constant use of popular communication tools such as Twitter, Facebook and texting, this is a generation that is equally as passionate about being an integral part of a team. To overlook this want diminishes their essential need for significance.

Because of their desire for dialogue they place a great value on interpersonal communications regarding career planning and performance feedback as well as enhanced corporate communications that give associates connectedness and relatedness. When there is honest, open and interactive communication managers are more likely to be seen as mentors and coaches which helps them to feel like someone above them is sincerely and personally concerned about their success.

- 89% want to have their ideas heard
- 82% would leave if their boss failed to value their opinions or ideas
- 81% want to feel respect

Compliance to standards is one thing but one's observations of any variance in adherence to rules will far outweigh printed company guidelines. In other words, a boss who fails to walk the talk will be viewed with little trust while one who has the capacity to model the behavior desired will be much more trusted. Contrary to some management's belief, Millennials actually like structure; what they dislike is those who profess it yet fail to follow it for themselves. It all contributes to their sense of trust.

- 88% want to work for a supervisor/manager whom they can trust
- 79% would leave their job if they were micromanaged

This generation's quest for collaboration and connectedness ties directly to their need for dialogue. Through engaging dialogue and sharing of knowledge and ideas, greater understanding evolves which enhances not only their work environment, but progress as well. Conversely, discourse and resistance to diverse thinking creates tension and blocks effective teaming.

This generation's number one value motivates them to be socially conscious backed by an intense drive to achieve results. This not only means that they are concerned about environmental and service-oriented issues, but also reflects their strong desire to be inclusive and respectful.

- They are competitive, but never ruthless.
- They genuinely value and care about other people and want to help others achieve as well as themselves.
- They relate to people at all levels and have a high regard for each person's contribution.

To leverage this strength requires inclusion and mutual respect from their leaders.

Leaders must be tolerant of new ideas and provide environments where employee input is regularly gathered and applied. Cultivating these new ideas is a competitive advantage in a world where competitive advantage cannot be sustained forever.

"Having a boss who I trust and who feels like they can trust me is invaluable to a job. Being treated like a child at work is very counter productive; eventually people will start acting like children if treated that way."

The environment of the new normal requires that the boss become more of a coach than a boss. And he/she better walk the talk.

Wanted: A More Likable Boss. One's likeability factor has served them well in nearly every realm of one's life, yet when it comes to being a boss, often that aspect is lost. With Millennials, it's an issue worth rethinking. The relationship between the boss and the employee is a critical issue for this generation. The old demanding, order-giving styles simply won't work. This generation wants less intense, more approachable managers; managers they can trust, respect and learn from. "A bad supervisor is like a Cancer. It kills my attitude, my performance and my ethics."

In today's competitive, fast-paced world managers must recognize that creating too many layers of decision-making may not bode well for achieving high engagement of employees. The dynamics of effective delegation and follow-up will become more important and will require some very specific shifts in style.

- 88% want a supervisor they can trust
- 89% want to have their ideas heard
- 81% want to feel respected
- 82% would leave their job if their boss failed to value their opinions or their ideas

The need couldn't be clearer; this generation wants to be a part of the decision-making process, wants to work with a boss they can trust and learn from and most of all, a boss who is approachable. That requires having a genuine likeability factor and establishing a strong and effective means of meaningful communication. Without it, you're doomed.

OWN IT:

- Understand that each generation differs in their values and communication preferences. Be aware and sensitive to these differences.

- There will be conflict as a result of generational differences. Don't make the mistake of taking this personally. Work hard at understanding the root cause of the conflict. Respect has a different meaning for different generations.
- Fear is a major factor in poor communication. Baby Boomers may feel threatened by the Millennials' expertise in technology. Millennials may fear the Baby Boomers experience and knowledge of services and products. Adjust your communication style when dealing with people of different ages.
- Focus on what you have in common with a different generation rather than how you differ.
- Blend the knowledge and insights that each generation has the opportunity to contribute.

CHAPTER SIXTEEN

From Assets to Ambassadors

Beyond Human Capital

Despite what is all too often heard from company leaders, it's not about capital. It's not about assets. It's about people, and people are not assets.

You can shuffle assets—changing them at will—but this does not work with people. Individuals are valued human beings who can contribute greatly to an organization's success when respected for their unique minds, distinct approaches, and specific ideas. No one understands a job better than the person doing the job—a fact that is many times ignored and replaced by a boss telling a person how to carry out his/her responsibilities. Not only is this wrong, it is also very demotivating.

When I coach and deliver keynote speeches I often speak about motivation. There are hundreds of books written on motivation—but I believe motivation is quite simple. Make people feel that what they do matters—that their work contributes to the success of the organization—and they will feel motivated. Plain and simple. People want to pride themselves on what they do, and many people identify themselves by what they do. That pride is visible to others and it becomes contagious. When this happens, these proud employees become ambassadors for the company's brand; they become the go-to people regardless of their titles. They speak well about the company and their co-workers and instill a sense of pride in others.

Ambassadors are also individuals whom I refer to as "underground leaders." Who are these underground leaders? They are the individuals whose roles allow him or her to influence others regardless of their official title. They don't necessarily manage others. They don't always have authority. But because of their dedication, superior performance, ability to collaborate and contribute, they are the "go to" people in their organization.

The most important advantage a company can have is to have ambassadors. Developing and supporting all levels of employees to become ambassadors is a mission all companies should embark on.

You cannot be an ambassador if you don't own what you do—and love it too.

Here's an example of one true ambassador:

> *Adam Sorensen is the Director of Engineering for a Silicon Valley manufacturer of printed circuit boards—one of the largest in the world. I've worked with Adam for several years during which he successfully grew into his present position. One of the reasons for Adam's growth is his "I own it" attitude.*

> *Recently Adam told me; "I'm very good at making circuit boards but that's not what defines me. I love making other people successful. Love to me is providing for my family and for myself. That's what I get out of it. That's what drives me. And everyone knows how I feel about my job and my company."*
> *Adam is a true ambassador for his company.*

Over the years I have discovered that ambassadors practice five I's of INGAGEMENT which are:

Involved: They are proactive about getting involved and often offer assistance or provide insights to help resolve issues in areas that they are familiar with but may not be under their specific domain.

Inquisitive: They seek knowledge and insights into information that can enhance their performance and the overall outcomes for the company.

Interested in others: They engage in conversations with co-workers, know how to ask questions and listen to learn.

Intuitive: They trust their instincts, combined with knowledge and experience.

Informed: They act as reporters and repeatedly ask questions—gather facts and details.

People who love what they do inadvertently become ambassadors. They tell anyone and everyone who will listen why they love what they do. They are the people you love to sit next to at a meeting or a party and whose sincere enthusiasm is contagious. Perhaps the most astonishing thing about ambassadors is that when the culture is aligned with their values, and their leaders support and reinforce their passion, both the employee and the company receive unimaginable blessings. A great example of this is the heartwarming letter that my longtime friend and client, Mack McIngvale, Founder and CEO of Gallery Furniture based in Houston, Texas received from a former employee one Thanksgiving:

Dear Mack:

I do not fear the man that can outsmart me. I only fear the man that can outwork me.

A setback is only a set-up for a comeback.

All things are difficult before they are easy. If it were easy everyone would be doing it.

Whatever you're going through, just keep going.

These are a few of the lessons I had the privilege of learning while under your leadership. Let me begin by first saying, thank you. The eight years that I spent working at Gallery Furniture changed my life. It was March 2004 when I started working for you. My life at the time was like an old country song. I had lost my job as a salesman at Landmark Chevrolet. I had not worked in three months. I was evicted from my high-rise apartment downtown, my new truck was repossessed and my girlfriend left me and took most of my friends with her. Then one day I received a phone call that would change my life forever.

I got a phone call from a guy that I worked with at Landmark. He told me that he had just been hired on at Gallery Furniture and that I should go apply. My first week at Gallery was not an easy one. Clock in at 7 a.m., unload trucks until 12 p.m., sell furniture until 6 p.m., deliver furniture until 1 a.m. and come back and do it again the next day. Not the kind of work I was used to as a salesman. But I felt good to be working again, and if the owner of the company can do it, then so should I. So I worked. And on my days off I would go in and make deliveries. I didn't take any days off for almost a year.

By this time I was spending more time on the sales floor. The following summer college kids came to work at Gallery. I had never thought about college before. I am embarrassed to say that I never graduated high school. Growing up, our role models were not Rhodes Scholars or Fortune 500 CEOs. Instead we idolized characters from movies such as Scarface or Good Fellas. College for kids like us was beyond our thought process. But then I remembered your words: If it were easy, everyone would do it. So, I decided to go to college.

I obtained a GED and started classes at Houston Community College. Two years later it was time to transfer to a four-year university. You may find this hard to believe, but before Gallery Furniture I could not name you three colleges in the state of Texas. I could never understand why people wore orange hats with a cow's head on them and I thought that A&M stood for automated teller machine. It was at Gallery that I learned what those emblems really meant and why people wore them proudly. I applied to three schools, the University of Texas, Texas A&M and the University of Houston. UT, because that's where you went and because Vince Young had just won the Rose Bowl, A&M because of the relationships that I had developed with the Gallery Furniture interns and UH because it was the school that the kids that worked fulltime or part-time at Gallery went to.

I did well at the community college. Well enough that I was accepted at all three schools. After much debate I chose to go to the University of Houston. I felt it necessary that I continue working at Gallery Furniture and a commute to UT or A&M from Houston three or four times a week just didn't seem reasonable, although I thought about it.

The courses at the University of Houston were a lot more demanding than I was accustomed to. At the time I was also writing training material for Gallery Furniture's Saturday morning meetings. I would work all day and study at night and go to school all day on my two days off. It was not an easy task, especially during finals and midterms. I was almost fired from Gallery on two occasions during finals week. I was spread out so thin between work and school that both sides suffered. But I would remember your words; whatever you're going through, just keep going. You are only as good as your last sale. So I would sale my way right back into a job. And at school I would remember, I do not fear the man that can outsmart me, I only fear the man that can outwork me. I would study for longer hours and often fall asleep in the library. I would wake up, take a shower in the recreational center and drive straight to work and after work drive straight to the library. It would have taken me five years to graduate from college, but my GPA had fallen to 3.3 and I didn't see that being competitive for what I had intended to do. So I changed my majors and continued forward. I graduated in 2011 with a Bachelors of Business Administration in accounting with an emphasis in internal audits.

I full heartedly feel that I could not have accomplished this without the support from the people at Gallery and your constant words of encouragement. Gallery Furniture was more than a job for me. When people find out that I worked at Gallery Furniture they often ask what it was like working for you. I tell them that working for "Mattress Mack" changed my life and I would not trade those years for anything.

Encourage, don't complain.
Persistence, tenacity, perseverance.
Over, under, through, but never around.
Face your problems head on.
You only fail when you stop trying.
It is not necessary to change.
Survival is not mandatory.
It is not enough to do your best, first you have to know what to do and then do your best. And the list goes on.

Thank you for all you do for your employees. Thank you for all that you do for the community and thank you for all that you have done for me.

May you have a prosperous holiday season.
HAPPY THANKSGIVING.

Sincerely,
Jorge Manuel Rodriguez

No. People are not capital nor are they a company's assets. People are valued human beings who when respected and valued for their unique skills, talents and individuality are the greatest ambassadors any company can hope to have. Regardless of one's position, be it leadership, management or staff, everyone has the opportunity to both be an ambassador and to influence ambassadorship. The choice is up to you.

OWN IT:

- How do you talk about your job? Do people envy you or feel sorry for you?
- It's not your status or your position that determines whether you can love what you do.
- What are you doing to create ambassadors in your organization?
- Write your own "Love What I Do" story and send it to me – engage@kabachnick.com. If you can't yet write your story PLEASE READ ON.

CHAPTER SEVENTEEN

Sometimes It's Time to Go

Just like in a relationship, sometimes the chemistry just isn't there. You feel as if you can no longer connect. You can't build relationships and you're frustrated by your co-workers' or your team's lack of energy. Your clock works with a sense of urgency that you don't believe others have. Try as you have you feel you're walking up the down escalator. It's been frustrating but now it's turning into resentment and possibly bordering on anger.

For many people, careers are not planned in advance; they simply happen because of opportunity, relationships, or luck. Have you relied on any of these to get to where you are today? How much control have you exercised over your career/job path?

Successful careers are created, not simply stumbled on. When you create a path for yourself you own that path. It's in your control not someone else's. You're the traffic cop. You are prepared for opportunities because you have planned for them. No one can tell you how you feel or what you love to do or don't. So how in touch are you with you?

You're Stuck so it Sucks

If you find yourself in a position of unhappiness are you staying because:

- You've just been there for so long that it's become ingrained—a habit?
- You feel no one will hire you because of your age?
- You can't afford to leave?
- You're intimidated by doing a job search?
- It's financially scary?
- You don't want to disappoint some people who rely on you?
- You're deluding yourself—it's really not that bad?

If for any of these reasons you choose to stay in the environment that makes you unhappy, that's your decision—unhealthy as that may be. However, I recommend you take action and ask yourself some tough questions in order to move your life to another level. A level of happiness where you enjoy your friends, your family, and the people you work with. Happiness is a choice, not a given. And to get there you first have to mentally fire yourself! Being totally honest with yourself, here are some tough questions to ask yourself:

- Do you enjoy coming to work as much as you enjoy going home?
- Can you picture yourself doing what you're doing a year from now?

- Give yourself a performance review. What ratings would you give yourself in your key responsibilities?
- Have you grown and developed skills recently? At what have you gotten better?
- Are you receiving acknowledgements for your contributions in the way you want to receive them?
- Are you still curious?

People who love what they do, leave a mark. I call it a mark or an imprint and not a legacy because legacy is too big to comprehend by most people—even those in executive positions. But every one of us will leave a mark. Large or small the mark you make will be imprinted on those you touch, work with, and live with. What mark will you leave?

Love what you do and you leave a mark on many. Hate what you do and you'll also leave a mark. Will the mark you leave be a beautiful star imprinted on someone's path through life or will it be a sad souvenir of what not to do? So before you make your final decision, do a reality check by asking yourself these soul-searching questions:

- Have you written down what you don't like about your job?
- Have you tried to negotiate a change in your job description?
- Have you looked into job advancement opportunities?
- Are you trying to find a better work-life balance?
- Are you too critical of yourself—focusing more on what you haven't done rather than on what you've accomplished?
- Have you recorded your accomplishments in a journal— manual or electronic?
- Have you identified your Values or Motivators? If you haven't then you don't know what to look for in the next company

you'll be looking at. (Go back to Chapter Four to review the importance of Values).

- Have you sought a mentor or coach to determine whether what you see or know about yourself is true?
- Have you asked for help from someone you trust to be brutally honest and give you feedback and advice before determining your next step?
- How do you look? Have you given up on your appearance because of how disenchanted you are about your job?

After doing a thorough reality check if you make the tough decision that it's time to move on, you'll start searching for your new beginning and to find a company and a position you believe you will enjoy. But before you can do that, a difficult and sometimes uncomfortable situation has to occur—the exit interview. Make the most of this situation by following these three rules:

#1. Be strong and brief. Begin by making it clear that you're not giving your notice so that your company can make a counter offer. Why put the company in a predicament to be embarrassed? They will think much higher of you if you begin the exit interview with that statement. It saves face for both.

#2. Don't lie about why you're leaving. Don't say, as most do, that you'll be getting more money—even if that may be true. That's a copout that will hurt the company by sending the wrong message. If the main reason for your leaving is your boss because he's a poor manager—look what you're doing by not telling the truth. You're putting others in the same situation to deal with this until they decide to leave. You don't have to undermine or make bad comments. Instead be prepared to state specific examples like, you feel you've stopped learning or you didn't feel you were provided with challenging opportunities.

#3. Say thank you. Mention a few things that you have learned and state that you are thankful for the opportunities that were provided. After all you were happy when you started this job. Don't forget the good before the bad began.

Learn from your past job experience so you will be able to better predict when you feel things are possibly not going well in your new job. Attack the problems when they first begin. Take ownership so you can love what you do and continue loving what you do. Passion for what you do leaves a mark on many people—especially the ones you care for deeply.

As you re-evaluate your situation it's important to remember that regardless of what you do—be it a job, a lifetime profession, personal endeavors or volunteerism, what's important is that you strive to be the best—give it your all with love and passion. Only then will you truly stand out and be seen as the person who is most respected and valued. I have a favorite saying:

BEFORE YOU BECOME FIRST – YOU
MUST BECOME BEST

I'd like to share with you a great example of what this saying represents for both a company and an individual:

The Richards Group – Stan Richards

The Richards Group is the largest independently owned branding and full service advertising agency in the country. Based in Dallas, The Richards Group reports annual billings approaching $1.25 billion.

I interviewed Stan Richards—Founder and CEO— a man now in his late 70's who looks like he's 60. Stan exercises everyday but he does a different exercise every day. He bikes, jogs, lifts weights, enjoys Pilates and yoga, and he often skis on weekends. I get exhausted just listening to Stan!

This is the culture Stan brought to The Richards Group and has been from the beginning. Here's how he explains it:

> "Our people stay. In an industry where high turnover is the norm, we are the exception. The average tenure of our principals is over 18 years. Ditto for our creative group heads. The fact is, when people join The Richards Group, many right out of school, they tend to stay. So when somebody gets to know your business, you know they'll be in it for a very long time."
>
> "We stay because our culture is one of respect for every individual in the company." As Richards puts it, "There are no unimportant people here." This explains why conference rooms are named for the people who have the longest tenure in the organization, from a traffic coordinator to a principal to a payroll coordinator. It's why everyone in the organization gets a bonus at the end of the year; why every significant purchase is weighed against the question, "Is it worth taking that money out of everyone's profit-sharing contribution this year?" It's why *The Dallas Morning News* named The Richards Group the Best Place to Work in Dallas-Fort Worth.

When I interviewed Stan and discussed passion and ownership with him he shared this story:

Stan played basketball in college and did quite well. Years later, while developing his business, he decided to coach a little league basketball team. Had a great team. Got to the championship game, then lost. Stan was devastated—absolutely crushed. How could this happen? The kids were crying—parents crying—everyone was unbelievably sad and upset.

Stan got home where he lives in the same community as all the kids on his team. He decided to mow the lawn; just to do something physical rather than just sit and think about losing the game and how everything went wrong. As he was mowing he saw his players down the street with their baseball mitts on, laughing, joking and playing baseball. They were having a great time. They had quickly forgotten their devastation. Basketball season was over and they had started practicing for baseball season.

Stan said he learned a very important lesson from the kids that day. Bad things happen—move on—but never forget to have passion—whatever it is that you're doing.

I asked Stan, "Can someone be successful without passion?" He thought for maybe fve seconds, looked me in the eye and confidently responded, "NO!" then added that he always reminds his team, "Do things with passion—unbridled enthusiasm. Distinguish yourself or go someplace else."

That's really what this book is all about. Helping you to determine what makes you happy; to identify what you love doing and what you have passion for. To discover how important it is to own it and to go forth with "unbridled enthusiasm." Isn't that, after all, something you'd like to be remembered for?

Pat Conroy (author of nine books, including *South of Broad*) was intereviewed for the CBS-TV show, 60 Minutes. The reporter asked him, "What do you want to be remembered for?" Without hesitation Pat answered, "I want to be remembered for writing passionately—truthfully—powerfully ..."

What do you want to be remembered for?